THE
WAY
OF THE
SHEPHERD

Living a Life of Surrender

Donna E. Lane, Ph.D.

Donna E. Lane, Ph.D.

Scripture quoted by permission.
Unless otherwise indicated, Scripture quotations are taken from the NET Bible® copyright ©1996, 2019 by Biblical Studies Press, L.L.C. http://netbible.com All rights reserved.
Scripture quotations marked (NIV) are taken from THE HOLY BIBLE, NEW INTERNATIONAL VERSION®, NIV® Copyright © 1973, 1978, 1984, 2011 by Biblica, Inc.® Used by permission. All rights reserved worldwide.

ISBN 979-8-9872527-0-3

©Copyright 2022 Donna E. Lane

All rights reserved. No part of this book may be reproduced in any manner whatsoever without written permission.

Table of Contents

Chapter 1 *Sheep-ish*   7
    What We Think We Know   10
    Our Best Efforts   12
    Our Deep Need   17
    Questions for Discussion   21
    Prayer   21

Chapter 2 *Knowing the Shepherd*   23
    The Character of Jesus   26
    Our Redeemer   29
    Equality with God   31
    In Jesus' Words   35
    Son of Man   38
    Son of God   41
    Questions   42
    Prayer   42

Chapter 3 *Knowing Ourselves*   43
    At War with Ourselves   45
    Pride and Humility   46
    Hope for Deliverance   49
    Battle Lines   52
    In the Vine   57
    Reflecting His Nature   59
    Questions   67
    Prayer   67

Chapter 4 *The Will of the Shepherd*   69
    As a Child   71
    Adulting   75
    Equipped   81
    Prepared   83
    God's Will   86

Questions 87
Prayer 87

Chapter 5 *Surrounded by Wolves* 89
    Serpents 92
    Doves 95
    Readiness 96
    Our Wolves 102
    Prayer 109
    One with Christ 111
    Questions 113
    Prayer 113

Chapter 6 *The Shepherd's Gifts* 115
    The Greatest Gift 117
    The Gift of a Father 121
    The Gift of Spiritual Fruit 122
    The Gifts of Beauty and Creativity 133
    The Gift of Truth 134
    The Gift of Freedom 136
    Questions 138
    Prayer 139

Chapter 7 *Following the Shepherd* 141
    Characteristics of a Follower 144
    Wisdom 150
    Cleaning House 154
    Surrendering into Dependence 158
    Questions 162
    Prayer 163

Chapter 8 *The Way of the Shepherd* 165
    Psalm 23 165
    Summary and Conclusion 185
    Questions 186
    Prayer 186

Acknowledgements

I want to express my deep appreciation to Connie Mitchell, my long-time editor, and Andie Newell, my long-time friend and prayer partner. Your contributions to this book are countless and immeasurable.

And for his continuous commentary and insightful feedback, reading chapter by chapter and keeping me on track—for this book and all my other books—along with undying support and belief in me, I want to express my deep gratitude and love to my husband, David Lane, my split-apart and the love of my life.

DEDICATION

To David
my fellow adventurer

SHEEP-ISH

"Has God not made the wisdom of the world foolish? For the foolishness of God is wiser than human wisdom, and the weakness of God is stronger than human strength" (I Corinthians 1:20b, 25).

I know nothing.

I'm a sheep. My entire worldview consists of my little corner of the field. My perspective is limited to whatever my five anemic senses perceive directly in front of me. I'm ruled by my bodily sensations and instincts without understanding beyond need.

A sheep knows nothing of skyscrapers, politics, airplanes, cancer, rock music, chocolate, or religion. Like a sheep, I can't even imagine all the things I don't know. No matter how smart I am (in animalistic terms), I couldn't possibly comprehend the vastness of the universe, the nature of God, or the complexities of the human heart.

I rely completely on my physical senses to gauge the safety of my environment. I wander through my field, oblivious to the dangers of cars on the nearby road or wolves in the woods or the cliff at its edge. I'm too sheep-ish to know who my enemies are. I'll run from my shepherd because he isn't a sheep, while I willingly approach the wolf because he's dressed in sheep's clothing.

I amble along with my head buried in the grass, not seeing the big hole two feet in front of me, and not knowing that if I fall in, I will die. In my mind, everything is fine. The grass tastes sweet. And since I have no knowledge of chocolate, I have no idea what I'm missing.

Yet, I'm arrogant and wild, willing to push against fences set up for my protection without thought to the consequences. I resent the shepherd's staff when it pulls me back from the edge and accuse him when his rescue hurts. And when I put myself in the wolf's line of fire, I blame the shepherd for the bites I receive.

I butt heads with my neighbors and stomp my hooves to prove my superiority or dominance, and sometimes just to be mean or aggressive. I'm quick to exclude those I perceive as lower in the hierarchy. Yet, I can be very passive in response to aggression from what I perceive as superior sheep.

I'm selfish and demanding, ravaging the ground designed to provide for me, and when nothing is left but dirt, I force my way onto the next plot of grass, only to decimate it—after all, as far as I'm concerned, my world is an endless green field for me to consume.

I stick close to my herd, but it's not based on love. I'm in it for survival, focused on what the next sheep can do for me. I'm often a follower of whatever sheep stands in front of me. Even if that sheep walks headlong into a ditch, I follow along blindly. I become terribly anxious when I'm alone, so I always hang with the herd and go where they go.

When faced with danger, I flee. I don't let anything get too close to me before I back away. I avoid dealing with problems at all costs. And I never walk a straight path, meandering through life without real direction beyond the drive of my instinct for survival.

No wonder I need a shepherd.

With all my sheep-ishness, my perceptions of myself and the world do not match the realities. It's as if I'm standing inches from a wall, staring at a small swatch smeared with paint. I can make out some colors—blue, a little white, and maybe a smudge of golden brown. I believe I see the whole picture and build my interpretation of its meaning based on the tiny corner I see. But I have no clue I'm looking at the Sistine Chapel. The beauty of the whole evades me because of the limits of my vision.

I'm like a two-dimensional creature trying to navigate a 3-D world—except it's an even more stark and profound limitation because creation is infinitely dimensional, and I'm trapped in my two. I'm missing too much information to function well.

My past is screened through an inner world swirling with fantasies, lies, and distortions. The future exists in imaginings built largely around those same distorted memories, with wishful thinking thrown in for good measure. My connection with the here-and-now is sporadic at best, interrupted by distractions, intrusions from my inner dialogue, and my propensity to live in the distorted past and imagined future.

And yet, I operate under the illusion that I'm in control. That I can handle life on my own. That I've got things figured out. I convince myself I have command of my life. I believe my perceptions are truth, my thoughts are accurate, and my feelings are valid.

I keep sliding along my two-dimensional path, believing I'm experiencing all there is to life. I babble nonsense about the unfairness of life while seeing a tiny fraction of the big picture. I wail and rage and shake my fist at God while my spiritual adversary chuckles, then barrels through my life unabated, wreaking havoc and stealing me blind.

Imagine this scenario—I'm an infant who's trying to act as CEO of a megacorporation, plunked down at the conference table during a hostile corporate takeover with the adversary sitting across the table from me. I believe I can negotiate to save my company, but

I don't know the language and can't possibly understand what's happening. It's not that I'm stupid. I would excel if measured by crying, sleeping, and suckling. I'm simply ill-equipped for the task.

What We Think We Know

Think back to when you were a teenager. Do you remember believing you knew everything and those stupid adults around you just didn't understand? The frontal lobe of your brain, the part involved in rational thought, problem-solving, empathy, planning and organizing to achieve a goal, motivation, decision-making, self-monitoring, insight, and impulse control, wasn't fully formed yet. You were missing some fairly significant pieces of information. But you knew better.

At least it *felt* like you knew better from the inside, based on the perceptions of your partially developed brain. Remember?

We are like those teenagers. We don't know enough to know what we don't know. Our five senses dominate our understanding of reality, so we miss the vast complexities of the unseen. We can't fully grasp abstract concepts like eternity, infinity, beauty, evil, faith, joy, trust—LOVE—beyond what we think and feel, which gives us a very limited view of these concepts and a restricted notion of reality.

Still, we race headlong through life as if what we perceive is all there is to know, rarely stopping to consider what's occurring beyond our senses. What stands as reality for us is reduced to the tangible and temporal. But like a teenager, we *feel* like we have a good grasp on reality. At least, it seems so from the inside.

On top of all that, we're taught how to act and what to believe from others who are as blind as we are. They, too, were led by blind guides, and so on, all the way back to Adam and Eve. Those beliefs color and distort our view of reality even further.

Perhaps we've been taught achievement equals acceptance, value, and worth. If we buy into this belief, when we fail, we feel shame. When we make a mistake, we believe we're worthless.

Or maybe we were taught the world is a dangerous place, so fear rules our decision-making process. Every bad thing that happens reinforces our belief. Instead of facing our fear, we shrink back and miss out on the wonderful redemption of growth in perseverance and character God provides from walking with him through suffering.

We may also learn hierarchy—the have's and the have not's, the greater and the lesser, the higher and the lower, the A students and the F students—where we measure ourselves by our position on the hierarchical ladder. Since someone else is always above us on this false hierarchy (even a record-holding Olympian knows someone will one day break their record, maybe even the next competitor), we readily believe we're not good enough.

The belief in hierarchy can mold us into either strivers or quitters, where we push beyond our limits, creating undue stress and pressure, or we give up, resigned that failure is inevitable. It can foster perfectionism ("I have to do it perfectly") and procrastination ("Since I'll never do it perfectly, I won't start").

Even our birth order can result in particular set of distorted beliefs. A firstborn can put more pressure on themselves because all the focus is on them to succeed, at least for a while. As a result, they may learn to take responsibility for others and believe, "It's all up to me." A middle child can often feel lost in the crowd. Since they can't keep up with their older sibling, "I'm never going to measure up" is a very common belief for the second-born child. The youngest child may get pampered by the older siblings and babied by the parents, coming away with a sense of entitlement and a view of themselves as the center of the universe.

These distorted views affect how we interpret our circumstances, which further colors our perceptions of reality. Beyond these common distortions, if we go through mistreatment, trauma, or loss, our worldviews are deeply impacted. For example, parental divorce or death can leave a child believing the loss is their fault. The sense of self-blame soon translates into anger and a tendency to blame others, including God.

Abuse in its many forms can result in the child feeling worthless, shameful, and unloved. They may learn to be hypervigilant, remaining on constant high alert for impending danger around every corner. They may question everything. 'What if' is a favorite question as they seek to protect themselves from future harm. The 'Why' question plagues them with frustration because no matter the answer, the reality of the abuse doesn't change. Doubt becomes their constant companion. Trust seems an impossibility.

These few examples are only a sampling of the misperceptions we can learn about ourselves, about life, and about God.

Suffice it to say, with all of these factors at play in us, how can we be certain of anything we think we know?

Our Best Efforts

To fully understand the destruction reliance on our knowledge brings, we must go all the way back to the story of the Garden of Eden. God placed two special trees in the center of the garden, a point-counterpoint presenting humanity with a choice. The first tree is called the tree of life. This tree is freely given, available to all at all times, its fruit unending. The second tree, the tree of knowledge, came with a restriction and a consequence. God said to partake of this tree means death.

But why would the tree of knowledge bring death? In Genesis, the tree is described as the knowledge of good and evil, which is a Hebraic expression meaning knowing good and bad or knowing happiness and misery—in other words, it refers to knowing everything there is to know, an all-encompassing knowledge. Operationally, this extent of knowledge tells me I have the ability to be the master (or god) of my own life, which is why the enemy said, "you will be like God."

Having the knowledge of God such that I believe I am the master of my own existence without having the full nature of God, and the wisdom, character, moral certainty, and perfect love his nature possesses, produces ultimate destruction. Notice the enemy didn't say you will become God. He said you will be *like* God or like a god. There is only one God. So, eating the fruit of the tree of knowledge didn't make Adam and Eve into gods. It left them believing they have the knowledge to be their own gods. What they didn't know is they didn't have the character to be their own gods.

You've heard the saying absolute power corrupts absolutely. While certainly true of human nature, this statement doesn't apply to God, whose perfect character is incorruptible. The same cannot be said of humanity. Instead of enlightening, the knowledge of good and evil corrupted. Adam and Eve thought being like a god would taste good. In reality, the knowledge was so devastating, God prohibited them from remaining in the garden with the tree of life, lest their lives turn into an eternal hell on earth.

This story is relevant to us now because we are presented with the same choice in our hearts on a daily, perhaps minute by minute basis. Will we choose the fruit of being gods of our own lives? Or will we choose humility, knowing God is God, and we are not? Will we surrender our will to God, or will we exert our will and try to determine the course and direction of our own lives, using our knowledge as the sole guide to our choices?

Unfortunately, due to the fallen nature of man, we're systematically trained from birth and reinforced through our experiences to believe we have to figure out how to navigate the world, to protect and defend ourselves, and to use *our knowledge* to determine the course of our lives. But *our knowledge deceives*.

Our knowledge tempts us to believe we can handle things ourselves. It convinces us we don't need saving but can save ourselves. It persuades us to listen to fear because we must be vigilant since it's up to us to protect and defend ourselves.

Knowledge entices us with the illusion of control, leading us to believe we can determine outcomes, that we can "make" others do what we want or "make" circumstances bend to our will. Since we believe we can handle things ourselves, then we want to make sure things are "under control." We buy into the illusion because we believe the alternative is being "out of control," which feels dangerous.

But out of control only exists if control exists, and control doesn't exist. There is no such thing as control. We make our *choices,* but those choices don't determine the outcomes or exert power over the choices of others. All we have is our ability to choose. Beyond our choice, infinite variables come into play which affect the outcome—other people's choices, random events, unexpected circumstances, unintended consequences, the actions of the enemy, and other existential factors can all have an impact on what proceeds from my choice.

When knowledge deceives us into believing we are in control, we become angry and bitter when our expectations of desired outcomes are not met. Then, when we finally admit we have no control in the external world, knowledge shifts our focus to within ourselves, telling us if we can't control others, at least we are in control of ourselves. This, too, is an illusion. Do you ever have random thoughts float up in your mind or stray feelings you can't explain? So do I. We all do. Those things are not under our "control." We can only choose what we will do with those thoughts and feelings when they arise.

Knowledge doesn't want to accept this truth because we think it means we are powerless, and to fulfill the mandate to figure everything out ourselves, knowledge desires power.

Knowledge also turns our eyes toward a hierarchical view of others, and our hearts toward judgment, directed toward ourselves and others. It feeds our pride *and* our shame. From Eden through today, reliance on human knowledge has been our downfall.

Think for a moment of all the Biblical stories where individuals relied on God and his truth—Noah, Abraham, Joseph, Esther, Shadrach, Meshach, Abednego, Daniel, Elijah at Mount Carmel, to name a few. Now, think of those stories where individuals relied on their own knowledge—Adam and Eve, Sarah, Saul, David with Bathsheba, most of Israel's kings, Judas, Peter at Jesus' arrest, Ananias and Sapphira, for example. What do these stories tell you?

Consistently, our so-called knowledge is unreliable and destructive, a set up for failure.

Despite the obvious failings of our best efforts, we double down, believing if we try harder, strive more, and just do it better, our strategies will work next time. But as the author of Ecclesiastes exclaims, "Everything is *hevel!*" (Ecclesiastes 1:2b). The word, *hevel*, means wind, breath, or vapor when taken literally, but is used metaphorically here to describe something transient, unsubstantial, and evanescent. In other words, our best efforts are no more substantive than a wisp of smoke blown away in the wind.

When we walk a path of our determination based on our knowledge, we are left lost and alone, stumbling in the darkness. In desperation, we reach out for anything we can find to ease the journey and make it substantive. Like the author of Ecclesiastes, we try relying on worldly anchors to stabilize our footing, but "the eye is never satisfied with seeing, nor is the ear ever content with hearing" (Ecclesiastes 1:8b).

Let's explore how the author of Ecclesiastes tried addressing *hevel* and what he found. I believe you may find some similarities to your own condition.

He tried creating accomplishments to build himself up—only to find they crumbled to dust or became meaningless over time (v. 1:12-15). After all, we can always go further, create better, accomplish more, right? When is it enough to satisfy? And where do we turn when everything we've created falls apart?

He built up his knowledge until he considered himself wise in the worldly sense, only to find his so-called knowledge brought him more frustration and heartache (v. 1:16-18). Perhaps he recognized how unreliable worldly knowledge is and how distorted human perspectives can be. And how do we assess the validity of worldly knowledge with nothing higher or greater to measure against? If all we know is what we know—and we know nothing—the reason for frustration and heartache becomes self-evident.

He reached for self-indulgent pleasures—what we might call pursuing the flesh—and declared them empty (v. 2:1-3). For while worldly pleasures might provide a distraction for a brief moment, the consequences we receive from their pursuit only worsen how we feel and add shame atop our disillusionment.

He tried amassing wealth and buying possessions but discovered they didn't satisfy his longing for something meaningful (v. 2:4-11). He couldn't get away from the fact that money and objects don't fill the deep need we have within for love and the emptiness we feel without it.

He sought satisfaction in the outgrowth of his labor but realized whatever he gained was going to be passed on to someone who didn't work for it—an "awful injustice" (v. 2:18-23). He also discovered his labor produced anxiety, frustration, and sleep disturbance. Worry and stress shorten an already short life and rob us of any hope of joy.

What's the point of it all?

His conclusion? Only God is the source of wisdom, knowledge, and joy (v. 2:26a). Every good thing in this life is a gift from God (v. 3:13). And, although everything else is *hevel,* "whatever God does will endure forever; nothing can be added to it, and nothing taken away from it" (v. 3:14).

When God provides us with Kingdom wisdom and the knowledge of truth, our eyes are truly opened. Like the blind man who Jesus healed in two stages, at first our perceptions may still be fuzzy, and we continue to misinterpret some things as he expands our awareness and feeds our hearts with truth.

But as we grow and deepen our reliance on him, our vision becomes clearer and our perceptions more accurate. We begin to understand and interpret circumstances through a Kingdom perspective. Our physical senses no longer limit our interpretations of our experiences. We transcend the worldly view and gain awareness and insight into the greater picture. We step back from the wall and see more of the painting.

Our deepening awareness of his profound love for us—not as a concept but as an experiential reality—fills us with joy. We become filled to overflowing with the fullness of God until we become as one. Our joy is fed by the beauty of his creation, the wonder of his love, and the glory of his presence within us.

Our Deep Need

Our deepest need is for the presence, guidance, and love of God—our shepherd who guards our hearts and leads our steps—our Father who loves us as his dear children, shares in our suffering, and saves us from ourselves.

Blessedly, God has provided for our deep need if we will receive what he offers. God's love is lavish, poured out in abundance, endless and never-failing. So, why do we often feel so empty and alone?

Perhaps you want to believe God loves you, but you've felt so unloved and unlovable throughout most of your life, you're having a hard time accepting he can love you. Or you might think he would love you if only you hadn't made so many mistakes in your life, but how can he love you, a sinner, at this point? Perhaps you're convinced he'll love you once you get it right or have done enough for him to please him. You might want to believe the Scriptural truth that he loves you, but it just won't seem to sink in. Or maybe you don't know what it means or how to immerse yourself in God's love.

To discover the depth of his love, you must first acknowledge your deep need. We must know and accept the depth and gravity of our need before we will accept what Jesus offers. If we continue to rely on our knowledge as we are programmed to do, we won't seek God's wisdom—why would we? We got this! After all, we believe it is all up to us and act according to that belief.

If we do acknowledge a need, we tend to get stuck on our need for salvation and allow our relationship with Jesus to stop there. We accept his great gift of forgiveness and redemption with thanks, then proceed to live our lives back under the weight of self-sufficiency and reliance on our knowledge. We consign God to a once or twice a week ritual of worship, and maybe a morning or mealtime prayer, without realizing what we're missing.

There is *so much more*.

When we accept Christ, "what is old has passed away—what is new has come" (II Corinthians 5:17b). Now, we must be "born again"—not in the traditional sense of receiving salvation. To be born again means the old ways must die in us so we can receive Christ's resurrection into a new way of life. We can't put new wine into old wineskins (Matthew 9:17). We must unlearn to make room for what we need to learn. With our whole hearts, we need to *surrender into dependence*.

What does it mean to surrender into dependence?

To surrender is to yield, to forego in favor of another, to give oneself up into the hands of another. In this case, it means to yield to God, to forego self in favor of God, and to give yourself over into his hands. Dependence in this context means reliance on someone or something else and includes the quality of trust.

So, surrendering into dependence is yielding your authority to God's authority, relinquishing your self-sufficiency and self-determination in exchange for his presence, guidance, and love, and trusting your life fully into his hands. It is complete, total release. To borrow an analogy from gambling, it means going "all in"—holding nothing back and keeping nothing aside for yourself.

We are asked to make a choice. Are we willing to surrender our illusion of control? Are we willing to submit ourselves to Christ? Once we make the free choice to be *willing*, the Holy Spirit can step in with power and help us in our inability. Love, wisdom, and truth are powerful—more powerful than our sinful nature and the lies we believe—when we receive them from God instead of settling for what the knowledge the world offers.

Like sheep who have gone astray (Isaiah 53:6, I Peter 2:25), we must return to the guardianship of our shepherd. But to do so, we must relinquish our position as our own savior, protector, and defender. We must let go of what we think we know and allow Jesus to replace our so-called knowledge with his tender love and care. Otherwise, we become prey for the predator.

Surrendering into dependence is a direct affront to the enemy and the sinful nature, so you will likely feel resistance in many forms. Fear may be stirred up that you will be vulnerable and exposed to hurt if you let down your guard. Shame may challenge your choice, claiming God can't possibly love you after all you've done wrong, all your many failings, and the extent of your sin.

You may feel like you're being asked to jump off the edge of a cliff without seeing how far you'll fall or if anyone is there to catch you, which to you will seem foolish. Satan will likely stir up doubt in God's goodness, his presence, and his ability to help you. Your pride may rear its ugly head and claim you can do it on your own—you're smart enough or cunning enough or skilled enough or good enough to make it without help.

Throughout the remainder of this book, I'll be addressing these challenges and offering direct responses to them based on Scriptural truth. We will examine the nature and identity of Jesus as our shepherd, and what it means for us to follow him. We'll also look at our natures, and the internal war that wages between the spirit and the flesh.

We will discuss the nature of God's protection and what it includes. We will refute all shame and explain how and why the cross has dealt with it once and for all. We will expose the root causes of fear and show how the resurrection obliterates the reason for fear while God's love casts it out.

We will acknowledge the foolishness of God's plan—from a worldly understanding—and talk about faith, its power, and its source. We will explore God's love and his truth in depth as our weapons in the internal battle. We will look at how Jesus deals with the enemy's weeds in our hearts to free up our spiritual fruit so we can grow and pour out toward others. We will discuss how to experience the full extent of God's love, as Paul desired for us.

Finally, we'll take on the sins of pride and judgment, and with it the desire for control—the root of all other sin.

In each chapter, I'll revisit the call to surrender into dependence, to acknowledge we know nothing, and to give our whole selves into God's hands.

So, we've come full circle, back to our awareness and acceptance that we know nothing. Living by human knowledge results in great frustration and heartache, as the writer of Ecclesiastes points out. We may think worldly knowledge will benefit us, perhaps even protect us from harm, strengthen us, or even save us, but what we find instead is emptiness. Nothing of the world can fill our hearts. No amount of human knowledge makes us whole.

But the Scriptures are filled with admonitions to seek knowledge of God and his ways. Jesus speaks to our lack of knowledge of God—and the only way to gain it. "No one knows the Son except the Father, and no one knows the Father except the Son and anyone to whom the Son decides to reveal him" (Matthew

11:27b). As Jesus says here, we know nothing, and at the end of the day, anything we know, we know because Jesus has revealed it to us.

So, what does Jesus reveal to us about the Father? Let's explore that question in the next chapter.

Questions for Discussion

1. In what ways has the illusion of control evidenced in your life? How has this desire for control impacted you?
2. What "sheep-ish" qualities do you recognize in your behaviors?
3. What beliefs have you been taught that have distorted your perceptions?
4. What similarities do you notice between yourself and the author of Ecclesiastes? Which of his attempts to deal with *hevel* have you tried? What conclusions did you draw?
5. Where have you struggled with surrendering into dependence on God? What have you been able to surrender into dependence on God?

Prayer

Dearest Lord Jesus, I invite you to be my shepherd. I am willing to align myself with your ways—but I can't do it on my own. I am willing to release my iron grip on control—but I need your help to open my hands. Please, Lord, cleanse my hands and purify my heart. Provide me with your wisdom and knowledge to replace my own. Help me to surrender to complete dependence on you. Reveal to me the depth of your love and prepare my heart to receive your love in its fullness. Thank you, Jesus, for who you are. Amen.

Donna E. Lane, Ph.D.

Knowing the Shepherd

> *"I am the good shepherd. The good shepherd lays down his life for the sheep. No one takes it away from me, but I lay it down of my own free will"* (John 10:11, 18a).

What was it about Jesus that prompted men and women to leave their jobs, their possessions, their families—their lives—to follow him?

In a parable that caused considerable controversy, accusations of demon possession, and threats of stoning, Jesus identified himself as the model shepherd, which he explains is the shepherd who willingly dies for the sake of his sheep. He contrasts the good shepherd to the thief, who sneaks into the sheepfold to steal or kill the sheep, and the hired hand, who runs when the wolves attack the sheep. Neither the thief nor the hired hand can claim the sheep as their own, but the good shepherd knows his sheep. They are his own, and they know the shepherd's voice and listen to him (John 10:1-31).

As I said at the end of the first chapter, what we know about God is whatever has been revealed to us by Jesus. So, what can we learn about the nature and character of God from this parable of Jesus as the good shepherd?

First and foremost, we can know he is *good*. He acts for the *good* of his sheep. If we dive into the meaning of the word *good*, we find additional descriptors we can apply to God, such as praiseworthy, moral, of highest worth, reliable, loyal, close (as in a close friend), kind, benevolent, virtuous, commendable, honorable, true, and of favorable character. His actions only benefit and never harm.

Do you believe God has these qualities? Do you trust him to act only for your benefit and to never cause you harm?

If you've believed, due to circumstances or misinterpretation, something other than God is *good*, it is important to stop and examine what has caused you to arrive at that belief, for whatever it is has come from the thief who desires only to steal, kill, and destroy.

As the body of Christ and his representatives in the world, we must take great care to examine our beliefs—and the *language* that we use—about God. Words have power. "The tongue is a fire…and is set on fire by hell. …it is a restless evil, full of deadly poison" (James 3:6, 8).

Some egregious misrepresentations of God have occurred because of our choices of words, some of them somewhat regularly. These poisonous words make it easy for nonbelievers, and even some believers, to come away with the conclusion that God is not good. For example, we are known to use inaccurate, unclear, or shallow language in reference to God's will, such as, "He *allowed* (the bad thing) to happen;" "He did (the bad thing) to grow you/teach you/get your attention;" and "God's ways are not our ways. We have to accept (the bad thing) is his will."

Do these explanations sound like God is *good*?

Scripture says every good and perfect gift comes from the Father (James 1:17). We are also told all things work together for good for those who love God (Romans 8:28). Now, these descriptions present God as *good*. But do you believe a *good* shepherd would send his sheep into a trench to get the sheep's attention? Would a *good* father allow his child to run into the road and get hit by a car to teach her to obey? Would a *good* shepherd willingly bring a wolf into the sheepfold?

Yet, in the absence of understanding the complexities of what we are discussing—or simply because we don't know what else to say—we can choose language without considering the far-reaching ramifications of those words. Wanting to help and grasping for answers in the midst of terrible circumstances, the body of Christ may resort to pat responses and dismissive platitudes instead of showing up with those suffering like Christ did.

Jesus got down into the mess with those who were suffering. He made space for their pain in his presence. He accepted the reality of pain and suffering in this fallen world instead of trying to deny it, avoid it, or fix it. He didn't cause bad things to happen, nor did he prevent bad things from happening. He didn't try to skip ahead past the difficult moments, and he didn't dwell back in time on past hurts. Instead, he showed up in the present pain and suffering with love, comfort, acceptance, and hope.

During those times when others are going through difficulty, it would be better to remind ourselves we know nothing than to offer simplistic platitudes that cause more harm than good. If we would choose to sit in silence with the sufferer, like Job's friends at the beginning of his suffering—before they started trying to make sense of the events based on their own knowledge—we would be demonstrating the heart of Christ.

Keep in mind that when Job's friends turned from being present to trying to rationalize, explain, and judge is when God found issue with them.

Bad things happen because it's a fallen world. Death is because of the fall. Pain is because of the fall. Hatred, disasters, sickness, suffering, trauma—all because of the fall. Do you recall how God gave clear instruction to Adam and Eve about the one fruit they were not allowed to eat? Would you then say it was his *will* that they ate it anyway? If so, he's a trickster and cruel, like an abusive parent who dangles the promise of cookies to entice their child to come to them, only to smack them across the face when they come. This is not God's heart.

God's will wasn't done in the garden, and God's will isn't always done on earth. Like Adam and Eve, when we choose contrary to God's will, bad things happen. As Scripture teaches, we reap what we sow (Galatians 6:7).

We can also receive the consequences of other people's poor choices, and the evil one and sin in the world can produce bad circumstances beyond our authority or responsibility. Yes, many things can cause bad things to happen, but *God does not*. God is *good*. There is no evil in him.

Does God have a role in this choice-consequence, reaping and sowing process?

Yes, he does. But it isn't to cause the bad things to happen. The consequences of our poor choices come based on the bad choices themselves. If I put my hand on a hot stove, I get burned. If I kick a soccer ball against the house and hit the window, I'll be replacing that window. If I spend the house payment on electronics and clothes, I'll soon be homeless. All choices have consequences. Some consequences are positive, and some are negative, but every choice produces a result. Every step on a path begins a journey to wherever that path leads.

So, what is God's role? How does he show up in our difficulties and suffering? What is the character of his response?

The Character of Jesus

In the parable of the good shepherd, Jesus reveals he is *present*. His presence provides love, comfort, peace, even joy in the midst of the struggle. The parable tells us he doesn't abandon us like the hired hand, so we never have to feel alone in our suffering. He makes a way for us to find pasture. His presence also provides his strength, his wisdom, and his weapons to prevent the enemy from using our circumstances to attack us with his deceptions, like the wolf who climbs over the fence to get to the sheep.

Notice how, in the parable, Jesus makes it clear the wolf *can* get into the sheepfold, just not by an honest path. In this way, Jesus demonstrates how everything that happens is not by his will, and the enemy does indeed come against us, even when we are with the good shepherd.

In addition, Jesus *knows* his sheep, and his sheep know and follow him. And because Jesus knows the Father and the Father knows him, we can also know the Father through Jesus. He goes before us to show us the good paths, and through relationship with him, we recognize him and know his voice so we can follow.

Knowing his sheep means he has invested himself in the relationship with us and sees our true nature. It takes a profound love to see beyond the flaws and rebellions of our sinful nature and recognize our true identity, often hidden behind a wall of muck and twisted vines of lies.

This is the depth of Christ's love—he sees into our true heart. And this is the kind of love he calls us to emulate toward each other. Without his help, we don't have eyes to see past the mire and find the true hearts of those around us, but with his eyes, we can see, and with his love flowing through us, we can follow the Kingdom ways of love.

Jesus calls us by name, which in Jewish culture of his time was of great significance since the name was believed to express the nature of the individual. Yeshua, for example, means to rescue or deliver. What an appropriate name for our savior! In the same way, Jesus changed Simon to Peter (rock) when he said he would build his church upon this rock, and Saul's name to Paul, which means humble. And like his name, Paul, the Pharisee of Pharisees, became humble, serving others for Christ.

Jesus knows us. Intimately. Completely. He knows the secret motives we keep hidden from others, and sometimes from ourselves.

He knows the random thoughts that plague us, and the random feelings that try to overtake us. He knows our dreams and our nightmares. He knows things we've never spoken aloud and the things we aren't even aware we believe.

And in the face of all those things—the good, the bad, and the ugly—he sees us as beautiful, holy and blameless, fearfully and wonderfully made. He sees a new creation. We are conquerors, victorious, filled with power and love. We are his beloved children, children of light and not darkness, a light for the world.

He sees himself in us.

We learn in the parable of Jesus' boundless *mercy* and lavish generosity. He is extravagant in his grace. He calls all sheep, even those from a different sheepfold, and brings them into the same pasture. And what could be more generous than giving up his own life?

As the good shepherd, Jesus *defends* his sheep, sacrificing his own life for the good of the sheep. His sacrifice reveals the extent of his love for us, that he would willingly lay down his life for our sakes. It also reveals his nature as a humble servant, the one who washes the feet of the disciples instead of taking his place at the head of the table and having them wash his feet—the one without any place to lay his head.

With the authority given to him by the will of his Father, Jesus stands against our enemy and fights him on our behalf. He never abandons us into the hands of the enemy and will never let anyone or anything snatch us from his hand. When we're willing to receive it, he empowers us with his authority as well, strengthening us to stand against the enemy's schemes with wisdom and truth.

Jesus also *leads* his sheep. The parable says he goes ahead of us, and he holds us in his hand. He provides the doorway to salvation and leads us into his rest. And like a shepherd who rescues his sheep when they fall into a hole, he is there when we struggle, willing and able to show us the way forward. He lifts us up and guides us through, by our side every step of the way, leading us into an abundant life.

Jesus *reveals* himself to us so we may know God. He reveals God to us in his actions, in his character, and through his love. And by his revelation, we are provided a clear image of what God desires for us—a life of love, joy, and peace, humility and service, sacrifice and relationship, goodness, generosity, mercy, and grace.

To have this quality of life, we need a shepherd. We need his presence. Without it, we live and die alone, for no one truly knows us. And we need to be known as only he can know us. He sees our genuine selves past the shrouding of the fall in a way no one else can. Seeing ourselves through his eyes is the only way we can know ourselves.

We need his mercy and grace because our failings are constant and many, and our lack of knowledge and understanding is vast. He looks past our failings and sees us as we are—tiny children in need of continuous care—no matter whether we understand our deep need or believe we have this life well in hand.

We need his protection and defense, for we live in a fallen world even as he has made us no longer a part of it. Our physical eyes are blind to the real dangers—threats to our soul. Without his defense, we make easy prey. We need his leading to navigate through suffering and difficulty, and to stay out of the numerous pitfalls when things appear to be going well.

We need his revelation, for without him showing us the face of God, we would have no concept of God's nature or character. And without knowing God, how can we love him? And without loving God, how can we put our faith and trust in him? And without putting our faith and trust in him, how can we follow him? And without following him, how can we believe in him? And without believing in him, how can we be saved?

Our Redeemer

God's main response to suffering and difficult circumstances in our lives flows from his identity as our *redeemer*. If we refer back to Romans 8:28, we see this response described. The bad thing may happen, but God works it for the good for those of us who love Christ. So, instead of God producing a bad circumstance to teach us or get our attention, he can—and does—redeem our bad circumstances and turn them for our good, which often teaches us, not only about his nature but about walking in his Kingdom ways.

A great example of God's redemption is found in Joseph's narrative. God redeemed Joseph's very sad story, filled with injustices and mistreatment and lies, by elevating Joseph into a high position and making it possible for Joseph to save his family and his people from famine. As Joseph points out, what was intended as evil against him to cause him harm, God meant for good (Genesis 50:20).

Job is another great Scriptural story illustrating this principle. Satan came after Job with both barrels—he lost his land, his possessions, his family, and finally his health. But in the midst of his worst suffering, Job said, "I know that my Redeemer lives, and that in the end he will stand on the earth" (Job 19:25).

I've wondered if Job was given a prophetic vision of Christ's coming and if in this phrase, he is referring to Jesus as the Redeemer who will stand on the earth in the end.

Job acknowledges God as his Redeemer *before* he redeems. But Job trusts and believes God will redeem. He has faith in the *goodness* of God. And, in fact, for Job, the redemption is full restoration.

Of course, Jesus himself is the ultimate story of God's redemption, the shepherd who lays down his life for his sheep and provides them a way to enter into the green pastures of eternal life, the greatest redemption of all. The Romans and the Jewish leaders intended the worst for Jesus—suffering the bloody stripes of the whip, the piercing pain of the crown of thorns, then the horrific violence of the cross until he died. But God turned the tables on them, redeeming it all unto salvation not only for the Jews but for all people. He brought life from death for Jesus, just like he brings life from death for us through Christ.

Do you see how, in everything he does and in every way he works in our lives, God is *good*?

Equality with God

Many verses in Scripture reveal the character of Christ, and through this revelation, the nature of God. One of the most beautiful and profound expositions on Christ's character is found in Philippians 2:5-11, where Paul expresses the *servant* nature of Christ as counter to the cultural values of this world.

It's helpful here to understand the environment in Philippi at the time Paul's letter was written. Rome was in the throes of the emperor cult, where the emperor demanded to be worshipped as a living god. In addition, the power-driven Roman culture valued status, wealth, advancement, and ambition over kindness, goodness, and care for their fellow human beings.

Some of the members of the church at Philippi were former Roman soldiers, accustomed to a high position and status, and many were Roman citizens. Prior to receiving Christ, they were devoted to the emperor and to Rome. Pride and control were the cultural norms. Can you see how their former values would clash with Christ's teachings?

As a result, the church at Philippi was struggling to accommodate for their new beliefs, resulting in conflict within. At the same time, they were coming under tremendous persecution from without. We can imagine how easy it would've been to go back to the values of the community in which they lived rather than face ridicule and imprisonment. Their innate pride worked against them also since pride came more in line with their culture's values than Christ's example.

Don't we face a similar choice in our culture? Our internal desire for control and our pride motivate us to achieve superiority, to gain more security at the expense of freedom, and to value things that give us the illusion of power, such as wealth or status or position. And like the Romans, our culture reinforces these beliefs constantly. Without vigilance and diligence, we easily slip back into the cultural norms around us and lose sight of our pursuit of Jesus' Kingdom ways.

Paul wrote the letter to the church at Philippi to address these problems. He clearly loved these people and had a deep connection with them. As he expressed in the letter, his concern was for their eternal state, urging them to hold onto "the word of life so that on the day of Christ (he) will have a reason to boast that (he) did not run in vain nor labor in vain" (Philippians 2:16).

So, Paul wrote the centerpiece of his letter to remind them of who they were to imitate in attitude and character. His presentation of Jesus' nature is in direct contrast and opposition to the attitude of the culture, which elevated man to the status of gods, valued pride, and desired control and power. Let's look at the stark contrast Paul presents.

> "You should have the same attitude toward one another
> that Christ Jesus had,
> who though he existed in the form of God
> did not regard equality with God
> as something to be grasped,
> but emptied himself
> by taking on the form of a slave,
> by looking like other men,
> and by sharing in human nature.
> He humbled himself,
> by becoming obedient to the point of death
> —even death on a cross!

> As a result God highly exalted him
> and gave him the name
> that is above every name,
> so that at the name of Jesus
> every knee will bow
> —in heaven and on earth and under the earth—
> and every tongue confess
> that Jesus Christ is Lord
> to the glory of God the Father" (Philippians 2:5-11).

What do these verses tell us about the character of Christ? Paul begins with Jesus' choice to empty himself. Although equal to God—remember Jesus' statement to the Jewish leaders that the Father and he are one in John 10:30—Jesus didn't cling to that equality, choosing instead to place limits on his divine nature. Compare that to the emperor cult, where the Roman emperor demanded to be worshipped as a god even though he wasn't. While still fully God, Jesus chose to take the form of a man—and not just any man, a slave. He expressed his human nature with his divine nature and became a servant, willingly by his own choice.

To better comprehend what emptying himself means, think about one of those many stories you've heard of a king or queen who goes among the people and lives as one of them. They are still the king or queen, so their essential nature hasn't changed, but they have emptied themselves of their position and status and privileges of being the ruler of the realm. To truly know the life of a citizen, the ruler would need to live the life of a citizen fully, including the full cost.

In the same way, Jesus did not give up his essential nature. He took the *form* of a slave. The Greek here doesn't indicate an exchange of this for that but refers to taking something in addition to what is already present. In other words, Jesus added humanity to his Godness. In doing so, he made it possible to truly live as a human so he would experience our lives, including the full cost, and so we would be able to know him fully.

What would it look like if we "emptied" ourselves? Rather than clinging to whatever status or position or power we've acquired, we would take the form of a servant to others. While retaining our essential nature—who God created us to be—we would think and act and live as a servant. We would choose to add a servant's nature to our own nature. Rather than seeking to elevate ourselves above others, we would humble ourselves before others and before God.

Which brings us to Paul's next point—Jesus operated in humility, and he did so in thought and action, even to death on the cross. Crucifixion was the most humiliating and debasing form of death known at the time, one reserved for the lowest of the low—so much so, Jews considered someone crucified to be cursed. Roman citizens couldn't be crucified because it was too debasing. Yet, Jesus chose it in obedience to God.

Other options were open to him. He could've skipped the whole come-to-earth-as-an-infant thing and gone straight to hell, battled Satan, and returned to earth victorious. He could've handled the whole bloody mess in the heavenlies without involving us in it at all. Instead, he went as far (and as low) as he could go. He entered our experience.

Rather than making his life about himself, he chose to make it about *relationship* with us. He desired understanding and empathy, and a shared experience, which are the foundations of relationship. Despite knowing he would be rejected and despised,
he wanted to connect with us and for us to connect with him.

He chose love and relationship over an easier road.

What would it look like if we chose humility, love, and relationship over easier, more palatable paths? How would our lives be different? Relationship means taking on incredible risk—risk of rejection, of loss, of mistreatment and pain—and choosing to love despite the consequences. It means tearing down our protective walls and false façades and opening up our hearts freely to others, even others who are not like us in looks or attitudes or beliefs.

Paul emphasizes Jesus' obedience to God, and how as a result of his obedience he was raised up and exalted. We must remember that Jesus didn't obey in order to be exalted. It wasn't a quid pro quo arrangement. Jesus was willing to let go of his equality with God—and did so. But Paul is showing us how God responds to obedience—meaning as we walk in alignment and agreement with God and allow our shepherd to guide our steps, God honors us and lifts us up into the heavenlies to become heirs of God and co-heirs with Christ.

In Jesus' Words

John 1:18b tells us, "The only one, himself God, who is in closest fellowship with the Father, has made God known." Jesus gives us a variety of descriptors to help us grasp who he is—the bread of life, the light of the world, the true vine, living water, and Son of Man, to name a few. Let's dig deeper into each saying and see what we can glean from them about his nature.

"I am the bread of life. The one who comes to me will never go hungry, and the one who believes in me will never be thirsty" (John 6:35b). In context, Jesus is comparing himself to manna in the wilderness as the Israelites fled Egypt, the bread from heaven. Manna was all the sustenance they needed. It was essential for their survival, was replenished daily, and was sufficient for each day. These, then, are descriptions of Jesus.

Jesus goes on to say, "The bread that I will give for the life of the world is my flesh" (John 6:51b), so the life his body provides is eternal life and its sustenance is for the spirit. Jesus is pointing ahead to the cross and connecting it with the Passover, when the blood of the Lamb of God and his broken body take away the sins of the world.

"I am the light of the world! The one who follows me will never walk in darkness, but will have the light of life" (John 8:12). In this statement, Jesus is claiming to be the only source of light, like the sun is for the planet. His truth illuminates and reveals so we can see the way to go, like a light in the darkness. Those who follow him walk in his light and never have to walk in darkness again.

He repeats his declaration that he is the light of the world as he is healing a blind man (John 9:5-7), and goes on to explain, "For judgment I have come into this world, so that those who do not see may gain their sight, and the ones who see may become blind." Again, Jesus refers to illumination—giving sight where there was none, and for those who claim to know without him, he reveals their blindness.

"I am the true vine and my Father is the gardener. Remain in me, and I will remain in you. Just as the branch cannot bear fruit by itself, unless it remains in the vine, so neither can you unless you remain in me. I am the vine; you are the branches. The one who remains in me—and I in him—bears much fruit, because apart from me you can accomplish nothing" (John 15:1, 4-5). Like the verses about being the bread of life and the light of the world, Jesus presents here another allegory identifying himself as the one source.

Just as a branch can't sustain itself without the vine, we can't bear fruit without being one with him. He is our one and only source, our sustenance, the life force within us. When we immerse ourselves in him, he feeds us and grows us. His Spirit flows directly into us, fills us, and makes us whole.

We can't attach ourselves to anything else without strangling our spirit. All the idols we rely on, like money, status, beauty, power, and control—and including self-protection, self-sufficiency, self-determination, and self-gratification—are poisonous, black streams flowing into our spirits and spreading disease until we lose our connection with who we are and with God.

The word translated "remain" here means to reside. We are to live in him as he lives in us. The parable hearkens back to his statement, "I am in the Father and the Father is in me" (John 10:38), as well as his teaching about the coming Holy Spirit, which explained, "You will know at that time that I am in my Father and you are in me and I am in you" (John 14:20).

The spiritual oneness Jesus describes between the Father and him, and he and us, is crucial to our understanding of who Jesus is. He makes it clear—separate from him, we accomplish nothing. Go back to my statement about Jesus' choice to make everything about *relationship* with us.

Do you see how each analogy presents a relationship? Bread enters the body and gives sustenance. Light shines, illuminates, and restores sight. The vine feeds the branches so they can bear fruit. We exist only in relationship with him. We cannot sustain, we cannot shine, we cannot bear fruit on our own.

Jesus uses a similar analogy when speaking with a Samaritan woman who came to retrieve water from Jacob's well. He asked her for water, but she questioned why a Jew would ask an unclean Samaritan woman for a drink. Jesus turns the tables on her and says if she knew God's gift, she would ask him for living water. Like us, she trusted her senses, and seeing that he had no bucket, she scoffed at him. Jesus responds by pointing out the limitations of her well water. Then he says, "But whoever drinks some of the water that I will give him will never be thirsty again, but the water that I will give him will become in him a fountain of water springing up to eternal life" (John 4:14-15).

Jesus described the living water as a gushing spring leaping up, not a passive puddle at the bottom of a well that you have to work to retrieve. Isn't that a beautiful image? No wonder the Samaritan woman was excited to receive some of his water. Like her, we're tired of trying. We're exhausted from the heavy labor of carrying the weight of life on our shoulders. The trying. The striving. The climbing. The hauling.

Who does Jesus say he is?

He says, "Come to me, all you who are weary and burdened, and I will give you rest. Take my yoke on you and learn from me, because I am gentle and humble in heart, and you will find rest for your souls. For my yoke is easy to bear, and my load is not hard to carry" (Matthew 11:28-30). He is rest. He is gentle with us. He is humble in heart, one who serves rather than demands to be served (Luke 22:27). He is the ease of a shared burden and the relief of a lighter load.

He is sustaining bread. He is illuminating light. He is the true vine—not the tangle of choking, parasitic vines of the enemy, but the vine that feeds and sustains our souls. He is a gushing spring of refreshing, living water pouring through us as we jump into his arms and receive his Kingdom.

Son of Man

Finally, and emphatically, Jesus says he is Messiah, the Son of God and the Son of Man. When asked directly if he was the Christ, the Son of the Blessed One, Jesus replied, "I am…and you will see the Son of Man sitting at the right hand of the Power and coming with the clouds of heaven" (Mark 14:62). But who is the Son of Man?

Jesus refers to himself as the Son of Man 81 times according to the NET. He is not called Son of Man by anyone else until Stephen witnessed the opening of heaven in Acts 7:56. The Book of Revelation has two references to the Son of Man, once among the golden lampstands and once seated on a cloud with a crown and sickle. Other than those instances, Jesus is the only one who uses this terminology to represent himself.

Most scholars believe the Son of Man refers back to a Messianic prophesy in Daniel 7:13-14, which states:

"I was watching in the night visions,
And with the clouds of the sky
one like a son of man was approaching.
He went up to the Ancient of Days
and was escorted before him.
To him was given ruling authority, honor, and sovereignty.
All peoples, nations, and language groups were serving him.
His authority is eternal and will not pass away.
His kingdom will not be destroyed."

Notice how the Son of Man in Daniel approaches the throne upon the clouds, like Jesus described. Did Daniel recognize Jesus in his vision as God expressing himself in human form? Was Daniel through prophesy identifying Jesus for us so we could recognize him?

Much theological debate has centered around these Daniel verses. Some question if Son of Man in this text is symbolic for Israel. Some suggest it refers to an angelic being. Some say the Son of Man and the Ancient of Days refer to the same being, since both are on the throne with ruling authority and sovereignty. Others interpret the text as pointing out the difference between the Son of Man and the Ancient of Days, which causes problems in the Jewish belief in monotheism, but lends itself to the Trinitarian belief in Christianity.

Despite the debate and unanswered questions, it seems clear when you compare the Daniel 7 verses with Jesus' description of himself as the Son of the Blessed One that Jesus was referring back to this Messianic prophecy to indicate his identity as Messiah, the Christ.

A crucial turning point occurred in Jesus' ministry when he asked the disciples, "Who do the people say that the Son of Man is?" (Matthew 16:13b). The offered various answers—Elijah, a prophet, John the Baptist reborn—but Jesus focused on the pressing question,

"But who do you say that I am?" (v. 15). Simon was the one who answered. "You are the Christ, the Son of the living God" (v. 16). Jesus called Simon blessed because God revealed the truth of Jesus' identity to him. Simon didn't figure it out on his own, and another person didn't say it to him. From that point forward, Jesus turned his face toward Jerusalem, and he began sharing what would happen to him there with the disciples.

Like Simon, we need God to reveal the true identity of Christ in our hearts. As I said before, what we know, we know because Jesus has revealed it to us. It's one thing to comprehend that Jesus is our savior, but it's another thing altogether to experience the revelation of his saving presence through the Holy Spirit in a personal, intimate way.

I can read that God loves me in Scripture and recognize the evidence of it in Christ's actions on the cross, but when Jesus reveals his love to me personally, it becomes tangible. His love transcends my mind and enters my heart, going beyond an idea to my experience.

When a painful circumstance enters my life, if I don't *know* God's love through revelation, I may still be convinced to believe the enemy's lies when he blames God or challenges God's love for me in the midst of my suffering. But if I've experienced his love firsthand, it's hard for the deceiver to convince me I'm not loved by God. I've received it, I've felt it, and I've embraced it. It is real to me.

Jesus called Simon blessed because he received the kind of personal revelation of Jesus' identity that left him knowing. Personal revelation from Jesus chases away doubt, "being sure of what we hope for, being convinced of what we do not see" (Hebrews 11:1b). This is the definition of faith.

The Son of Man came to serve and to give his life as a ransom for ours (Mark 10:45). He chose to do so personally, intimately, to share himself with us and reveal God's nature through relationship with us. He chose this path when other ways were available to him. Why? I believe he desires to pour out his love on us in a tangible way, and this path allowed us to share in the experience of his love.

Since this was his choice and his desire, let's not settle for our own "knowledge" (what we think we know) as sufficient. Let's seek revelation from Jesus so we may experience the spring of his living water bursting forth and leaping up in us from the depths of our hearts.

Son of God

So, who is this Messiah? What is he all about? According to the prophesy in Ezekiel 34:11-31, he gathers and rescues his scattered sheep. He seeks those lost and returns those who stray. He feeds his sheep on the mountains and by the streams. He makes his sheep lie down in lush pastures and feeds them rich grass. He bandages the wounded sheep and strengthens the sickly sheep. His sheep are no longer prey for wild beasts because he personally watches over them. He is their one true shepherd.

He makes it possible for his sheep to live without fear. He showers them with blessings and much fruit. He breaks the bars of their yokes and rescues them from enslavement to their oppressors. He doesn't allow injustices to stand but personally judges those who trample their pastures and thrust their horns at his sheep. And he establishes a covenant of peace with his sheep, which he personally oversees.

He is actively engaged and personally involved in every aspect of the lives of his sheep.

What beautiful imagery of the goodness, the sacrifice, the leading, the service, the humility, and the redeeming nature of the shepherd. He is the bread that feeds our soul, the living water that fills our spirit, the light that gives sight and guides our feet to better paths, and the vine in which we abide as one. He is the Son of Man and the Son of God, fully sharing in our experience of humanity and fully sharing his deity with us.

His covenant of peace is everlasting.

Questions
1. In what specific ways has God shown you that he is *good*?
2. How has God's nature been misrepresented to you so that you questioned his goodness? How have you misrepresented God to others in the past?
3. How have you experienced God's *presence* in your life? God's *leading*? God's *mercy*? God's *defense*? God's *revelation*? God *knowing* you and you knowing him? God's *redemption*?
4. In what areas of your life might you need help to humble yourself and empty yourself in imitation of the character of Christ?
5. Who do you say Jesus is? What qualities of Jesus are you able to see in yourself? (If you are unsure, ask Jesus to reveal how he sees you).

Prayer

Precious Lord, thank you. Thank you for revealing the nature and character of God to us in such a tangible way. Thank you for humbling yourself willingly to take on our humanity so we might share in your deity. Jesus, help me to always keep in the forefront of my mind your goodness and to continuously look for your redemptions. Please provide more and more revelations of your nature so I may know you. Fill me with your living water until it bursts forth to overflowing. Feed my soul with your bread. Open my eyes with your light. And Lord, help me to always remain one with you, abiding in the vine. Let me know the full extent of your love for me, so that when the enemy comes to stir doubt, I am able to answer without question with who I know you to be. Thank you, Jesus, for being you. Amen.

KNOWING OURSELVES

"O LORD, you examine me and know me. Certainly you made my mind and heart; you wove me together in my mother's womb" (Psalm 139:1,13).

How can art see and understand itself—except through the eyes of the artist?

From our inception, God's fingers are intimately involved in our design. He weaves our DNA and constructs our genetic code, then merges chosen aspects of his Spirit into an inimitable combination, creating a masterpiece of unique splendor for a specific purpose. It is a labor of love.

His wonderful creation, fashioned precisely according to his will, comes into this world, and almost immediately, the taint of the fall begins its relentless shrouding. Perhaps our overtaxed parents, stressed by our nonstop 3 am screams, don't know how to respond to our discomfort, and we learn not to trust. Maybe a jealous older sibling mistreats us, and we learn to fear. Or possibly we receive harsh correction for our misbehavior and learn shame. Certainly, bad events or circumstances will happen to all of us because of the fallen nature of the world. We tend to interpret those bad things as reflections on us instead of results of the fall.

Before long, the shroud hides our true nature from our eyes. We can begin to believe we are bad, unworthy, and unloved. We feel an absence of value, meaning, substance, purpose, and strength to face our fears. Insecurity leads to inferiority as we begin to judge others as we judge ourselves.

Once obscured under the covering of lies, how can we understand our true identity?

We can't. The only one who knows us—and our only source to know ourselves—is God. Without God's revelation of our nature, we remain shrouded in darkness. Uncertainty and doubt are our constant companions.

We can study dominant and recessive gene combinations and understand things like eye color and height from a scientific perspective. We can take human-made personality assessments and enneagram tests to try to make sense of how we act. But because God interweaves elements of his Spirit into our creation, we can't understand who we are without first knowing the character and nature of God. In the last chapter, I discussed in depth what Jesus reveals to us about God's nature. Once we receive this revelation through our relationship with Christ, we are in a much better position to understand his revelation of who we are.

Unfortunately, the same insecurity, uncertainty, and doubt that comes from the fall pushes us to seek control. The more we try to control, the more out of control we feel, so the stronger our desire for control becomes. This vicious cycle makes it increasingly difficult for us to seek God or surrender into dependence on him. Cut off from our only source, we turn to reliance on our own knowledge and understanding, which only increases our blindness and fuels our pride.

Pride expresses through a sense of superiority, but that presentation is deceptive, because pride is actually an overcompensation for a sense of lack. What is it we fear we lack? Substance. Value. Worth. Meaning. Purpose. Strength. *Identity*. Pride covers up that fear and hides it deep in dark wells within us. We deceive ourselves that those feelings are gone—but the churning rumblings of fear never go away.

Thus, because of the fall, all of us exhibit some degree of narcissism. To be clear, I'm not referring to the few who have the extreme narcissism that is severe enough to be diagnosed as a personality disorder. But narcissism exists on a continuum, and all of us land somewhere on that continuum, because all of us have a problem with pride.

Narcissism comes in two forms: grandiose and vulnerable. Grandiose narcissists appear superior and act as if they are more important than others. They tend to be arrogant and assertive in how they present themselves. Vulnerable narcissists, by contrast, appear needy, clinging, and anxious. They tend to be self-debasing. However, both types are self-centered, entitled, and antagonistic toward others in different ways.

The unexpected cause of narcissism is insecurity. It's as if we are constantly puffing up a balloon to cover up the leak in it. What looks like grandiosity is actually compensation for our perceived lack of substance and worth. Paradoxically, the focus on compensating for our insecurity—the constant puffing up of our balloon—means we are completely self-absorbed.

And despite puffing ourselves up before others, on the inside we can't ignore the hissing evidence of our lack.

Along with our deep insecurity comes self-doubt—and no wonder we have self-doubt. We know nothing. We're wanderers in the darkness, blind to our next step. Our cloak of pride may hide our sense of inferiority for a time. But we've built our houses on sand. A breath of wind shakes us to our core. We're washed out to sea at our next misstep when a wave of self-doubt overtakes us. The very thing we rely on to make ourselves feel more secure is itself an insecure foundation.

At War with Ourselves

So, we have an intrinsic need. Just like an infant trying to figure out how to navigate life or a sheep trying to survive in a hostile world, we desperately need a guardian—a shepherd to watch over us, to protect us, to lead us, to teach us, and to care for us. This need is at war with our innate desire to do it ourselves, to have our own way—to buy into the control illusion.

We're ripped in two, "a double-minded individual, unstable in all [our] ways" (James 1:8). Our flesh or desire to be our own god is at war with our spirit, but both can't coexist. One must submit to the other. We're like England and Germany in our own internal World War, blitzing each other with bombs of shame, fear, and self-debasement in an attempt to gain dominance over the other side.

It's strange, isn't it? We desire wisdom, yet we keep a tenacious hold on our own perspectives in the deep places in our hearts and doubt everything that doesn't agree with our feelings in the moment.

We long to be righteous but continue to pursue the cravings of our flesh, as if we don't have a choice but to give in to our passions.

We want so badly to be loved and cared for, and when we're not, we're wounded by the bombshells of rejection and abandonment, while at the same time, we don't want to need anybody. We don't want to be vulnerable. We cling to our self-protection and our self-sufficiency. Safety and security become our highest values instead of love.

So, the very things we want—wisdom and righteousness and love—we refuse or sabotage with our insistence on control.

I always say, where there's a problem, control is at the heart of it.

Pride and Humility

Scripture offers a description of our inner World War. "Is [conflict] not from this, from your passions that battle inside you? You desire and you do not have…You do not have because you do not ask; you ask and do not receive because you ask wrongly…Adulterers, do you not know that friendship with the world means hostility toward God?" (James 4:1b-2a, 3a, 4).

James goes on to offer a resolution to the inner conflict. "God opposes the proud, but he gives grace to the humble. So submit to God. But resist the devil and he will flee from you. Draw near to God and he will draw near to you. Cleanse your hands, you sinners, and make your hearts pure, you double-minded" (James 4:6b-8).

Let's go a little deeper into these verses to better understand what James is saying to us. The Scripture in James 4:6b ("God opposes the proud, but he gives grace to the humble") references Proverbs 3:34, which reads, "With arrogant scoffers he is scornful, yet he shows favor to the humble." This verse in Proverbs is sandwiched between two similar verses, the first about the wicked vs. the righteous, and the second about the wise vs. fools. In each case, God's blessing and honor is upon one character trait and his contempt is on the opposing trait.

The Proverbs verse indicates that pride and doubt go hand in hand—which makes perfect sense. To doubt the all-knowing God, I would have to believe I know more than he does. Why else would I cling to my own perceptions, thoughts, and feelings over his words? Otherwise, I would believe him without question. Of course. Why wouldn't I? He's all-knowing. The verse goes on to elevate humility, which means acknowledging I do *not* know—in other words, knowing that God is God, and I am not.

James' solution to pride and doubt is submission to God. The Greek word here is a form of the word used in several places in the New Testament (such as "submitting to one another" in Ephesians 5:21) which indicates placing or arranging yourself in alignment or abiding with. The Hebrew equivalent word means to serve, to present yourself, or to bring near. So, we are to present ourselves and bring ourselves near to God and align ourselves with his ways—the ways of the Kingdom as opposed to the ways of the world. For, as James says, "friendship with the world means hostility toward God (James 4:4b).

James further instructs us to resist Satan, indicating that pride and doubt are not just of the world, they are of the enemy. This verse includes a promise—"he will flee from you" (v. 7). The promise here is if we humble ourselves (acknowledge we do not know) and refuse to entertain the enemy's questioning whispers because we are trusting the all-knowing God and not our own understanding, Satan will slither away from us like the snake he is, because we are refusing to give him permission to remain—and he can't harass us without our agreement.

At the same time, as we draw near to God, our awareness of God's presence rekindles something within us, the part of our hearts that desires wisdom and righteousness and love. In choosing to draw near to God and align our spirit with his, his Spirit in us lifts us out of our flesh and restores us into the Kingdom life.

Two more instructions remain in these verses. The first is to cleanse our hands. Why would James focus specifically on the hands? Because it is with our hands that we grasp and hold. Our grubby little infant hands don't want to let go of the illusion of control.

We like believing we're in control, don't we?

We think it makes us powerful, which means we won't be overpowered. We like to feel important. It's a false and impotent way to contradict the distortions we've been taught that tell us we don't matter. We don't want to let go and put our trust in God because fear has convinced us we're safer in charge.

What we don't see is the filth that coats our hands because we have a vise grip on our obsession with control and it's many offshoots. We must open our hands to clean them, which means letting go of our arrogance, our need for power and superiority, our self-protection, and our desire for control. Only through our willingness to release our grip and surrender into God's hands can God cleanse our hands.

The second instruction is to purify our hearts. The battle between our two minds—the part that desires wisdom, righteousness and love, and the part that clings to our pride, our fleshly passions, and worldly desires—takes place in our hearts. The root of control leaves our hearts vulnerable to other deceptions from the enemy. As a result, he plants the seeds of his lies early and often in our lives. His seeds sown in our hearts feed off the deep root of control and grow to form constricting vines that tangle around each other until they become a stifling, engulfing mass. They must be rooted out like weeds from the garden. Otherwise, they squeeze out and overgrow the good seeds of wisdom, righteousness, and love, sucking up all our resources, and we never produce the fruit God desires.

Our willingness for God to heal our double mindedness frees him to act on our behalf, digging up Satan's lies and replanting our hearts with truth. Admittedly, this process of plowing, tilling, and harrowing the soil of our hearts, leveling the field, and digging deep to plant new truth can be difficult and painful. But consider the alternative—continuing to be your own worst enemy in an internal fight that tears you apart for the rest of your days.

Ask yourself this. If you had a deep, gaping cut, would you go to the doctor and have him clean out and stitch up your wound, or do you let it fester until you have no choice but to cut off your leg—or wait until it kills you? Of course, cleaning out the wound hurts. Yes, the healing process takes time and leaves you raw and aching. But it's worth it because, ultimately, it makes you whole.

Short-term pain for long-term gain is a mature, wise choice, so our sheep-ish selves will need our shepherd's help to choose it. We are much like a child who cries because she doesn't want to go to the doctor or doesn't want to eat vegetables. She isn't thinking about the long-term consequences of her choice. Her motive is to avoid the fear of the doctor's visit or the taste of the vegetables.

But the good, loving parent takes her to the doctor for her checkup and encourages her to eat her veggies anyway, knowing the long-term consequences and the big picture and wanting only the best for her.

Hope for Deliverance

Paul talks at length about his personal battle between the flesh or sin nature and the spirit.

"I do not understand what I do. For what I want to do I do not do, but what I hate I do. And if I do what I do not want to do, I agree that the law is good. As it is, it is no longer I myself who do it, but it is sin living in me. For I know that good itself does not dwell in me, that is, in my sinful nature. For I have the desire to do what is good, but I cannot carry it out. For I do not do the good I want to do, but the evil I do not want to do—this I keep on doing. Now if I do what I do not want to do, it is no longer I who do it, but it is sin living in me that does it.
So I find this law at work: Although I want to do good, evil is right there with me. For in my inner being I delight in God's law; but I see another law at work in me, waging war against the law of my mind and making me a prisoner of the law of sin at work within me. What a wretched man I am! Who will rescue me from this body that is subject to death? Thanks be to God, who delivers me through Jesus Christ our Lord! (Romans 7:15-24 NIV).

Paul begins this section as I began this book—with an admission that he doesn't know. He doesn't understand what he's doing. His spirit desires God's way, so why can't he pull it off? Paul answers his own question—his sinful nature is the problem. Paul is saying the sin living in him—the lies embedded deep within—battle against what he desires in his spirit, leaving him divided and at war with himself.

Like James, Paul recognizes his only hope for deliverance from what he terms "this body that is subject to death" is Jesus Christ. Paul goes on to describe how Jesus has made it possible to "walk according to the Spirit…if indeed the Spirit of God lives in you" (Romans 8:4b, 9b). When we align ourselves with Jesus, who lives in us, we are walking according to the Spirit. And when we walk according to the Spirit and the truth begins to inhabit our hearts, the lies begin to lose their strangle hold.

Paul also acknowledges our sheep-ish need for help, saying "the Spirit helps us in our weakness" (Romans 8:26a). Remember, we know nothing. We're infants in a hostile world. We're wandering sheep. Without Christ's help, we cannot hope to win this internal battle—like Paul, we can't pull it off on our own.

We can't live according to the Spirit and according to the flesh. They are contrary and opposed to one another. It's like trying to breathe and swallow at the same time. We either suffocate or choke on whatever we're trying to swallow. Or it's like trying to fight on both sides in a war at the same time. Nothing comes from it but our destruction. As Paul states,

> "For those who live according to the flesh have their outlook shaped by the things of the flesh, but those who live according to the Spirit have their outlook shaped by the things of the Spirit. For the outlook of the flesh is death, but the outlook of the Spirit is life and peace, because the outlook of the flesh is hostile to God, for it does not submit to the law of God, nor is it able to do so" (Romans 8:5-7).

It isn't by our own effort that we put the flesh to death. According to Paul, it is "by the Spirit" that the flesh is put to death (Romans 8:13b). Our role includes willingness, choice, and surrender. These are the question we must answer—

> Are we willing for the Spirit to take authority over our flesh?
> Will we choose to open our hands and let go of control?
> Will we surrender our will to his?

I struggled for many years with the belief that my knowledge could save me. I thought, through vigilance and control, I could manage any hardship or struggle, including my destructive internal dialogue. After all, I had studied psychology. I knew how all that stuff worked. Right?

Wrong.

All the cognitive weightlifting in the world couldn't overcome the lies I believed about myself and about God. It wasn't until my internal misery left me face down on the floor and I surrendered to God that the darkness began to lift. When I told him I was willing for him to take over the battle, I could feel the oppression lighten. When I chose to want to let go of my intelligence as my savior, my vigilance as my protection, and control as my god, he stepped in with *truth*, which ousted the enemy and shielded me from his attacks. And when I surrendered my will into his hands, he took my hand, stood me up, and enveloped me in *love*. For the first time, I knew I was loved, and I felt worth loving.

If we are willing, we choose, and we surrender to the Lord, Jesus will deliver us.

Battle Lines

In the benediction of Hebrews, the author refers to Jesus as "the great shepherd of the sheep" (Hebrews 13:20b). It is within that context that the author indicates Jesus equips us with everything we need to do God's will and works within us for us to be pleasing to God (v. 21). The two main things we need, and that Jesus provides in abundance, are *love* and *truth*.

Let's revisit the internal World War analogy. Visualize the battle line. The armies of the enemy are dug in. They have established strongholds throughout the area. Their trenches provide deep, intricate, and intertwining webs of protection for them to hold their position. Because they have strengthened their position through years of deception reinforcing deception, they have layers of shielding before we can get to their command center.

Their weapons are the lies of control and judgment, including pride in all its forms. Each weapon fuels and reinforces the other weapons until the enemy weaves an impenetrable wall, behind which our true, God-given nature—our spirit which desires wisdom, righteousness, and love—is held prisoner.

Now, let's look at the other side of the battle line. What do we have to stand on? What weapons do we use in the fight? Our intelligence? Oh, how our enemy loves it when we rely on our own understanding. When we do, we make it incredibly easy for our enemy to deceive us, because our understanding doesn't have any foundation beyond what we *think* we know, and our perceptions, as I've discussed, are both limited and distorted. If our intelligence is our strength, how quickly we're devastated when we find out we were wrong—about anything. And only pride would try to convince us we're never wrong.

OK, so not intelligence. What about self-confidence? If we have adequate confidence, wouldn't that give us good ground from which to fight? On the surface, it sounds like that might work—that is, until the enemy condemns us for our inevitable failures and erodes our confidence because it's built on a false foundation of successful outcomes. Instead of being a rock, our confidence based on success is sinking sand, easily washed away by a turn in our circumstances. In fact, the more we place our confidence in ourselves, the more we realize our confidence is misplaced.

If we rule out self-confidence because of its fragility, what about self-esteem? Psychology talks a lot about the importance of high self-esteem. Surely that would provide us a strong position in the battle. But what do we base our self-esteem upon? Do we rely on feedback from others to build our self-image? If so, the feedback of others will also have the power to destroy it.

Do we rely on words of affirmation to build us up? Words of affirmation are great tools for building upon a strong foundation, but if we don't already have a good foundation established, it's difficult to receive the words of affirmation, and our building will crumble at the first storm. And what do we base our words of affirmation on? The opinions of others? How can we know if those opinions are reliable? People are notorious for projecting their beliefs about themselves onto others, so it's possible, even likely, that any words coming from others are more about the speaker than about us.

Do we base our words of affirmation on general concepts that apply to everyone? Those ideas may be true, but since they aren't personal or connected to anything specific about us, they lack the import to overcome the targeted lies of the enemy. Do we base our affirmations on our own opinions? Our opinions, when based on our own understanding, are no more valid than the opinions of others. No, we need something more than words of affirmation.

Do we rely on our achievements? Our job? Our looks? Our social status? The number of followers we have on social media? All of these weapons are insecure, temporary, and transient, so when they disappear, so does our self-esteem. Not a great strategy, to rely on a weapon that can vanish in an instant at someone else's whim.

How about our goodness? If we try hard enough to be good—if we strive for perfection—wouldn't that be solid ground? Can we be "good enough" to overcome the enemy's weapons against us? Keep in mind, Israel tried for more than 1500 years to achieve perfection in following the ways of God by following his law—and failed. Even the disciples, having known Christ, couldn't manage to get it right when they tried in their own strength. Do we believe we'll have a better outcome than they did? If a random thought floating up from our unconscious mind can betray us and steal our illusion of goodness, then it seems a poor choice of ground from which to fight.

What about our ability to love? While it's true that love is a powerful weapon, in our feeble hands love can become conditional, an economy of exchange, dependence and neediness, or a tool for manipulation and guilt—in other words, not love at all. Only *perfect* love casts out fear (I John 4:18), and we are anything but perfect in our expressions of love. Every failing in our love becomes a gap in our battle line where the enemy can pour through with condemnation, fear, and self-degradation.

Can we agree, then, that on our own, without any solid ground to stand on, we can't win this internal battle? It's as if we are using BB guns to fight against a nuclear arsenal. No wonder the enemy's lies *seem* to have so much power. We are like sheep at the mercy of the wolves without our shepherd.

Paul explained, "For our struggle is not against flesh and blood, but against the rulers, against the powers, against the world rulers of this darkness, against the spiritual forces of evil in the heavens. For this reason, take up the full armor of God so that you may be able to stand your ground on the evil day, and having done everything, to stand" (Ephesians 6:12-13). Using weapons of the world against the spiritual forces of darkness and evil is futile.

Any good general will tell you to take a battle position on the high ground if you want to win the engagement. Our spiritual high ground is, paradoxically, a place of surrender, aligning ourselves with God and submitting to his authority and power, relinquishing our own weapons in exchange for the armor that he provides (Ephesians 6:14-17).

His armor includes *his* truth which the Holy Spirit speaks to our hearts, *his* righteousness afforded to us by his blood, *his* peace in our hearts provided by his presence within us, *his* faith so we may believe and act to quench enemy fire, *his* salvation established by his death on the cross and resurrection, and the *gladius* (a weapon used for offense/attack in close hand-to-hand combat) of *his* Spirit.

For it is his Spirit who overcomes. We need him to provide the two things we need—*love* and *truth*. We need him to fight the battle as we surrender into dependence on him. We need his power to strengthen us in our weakness.

Note that all the weapons effective in the battle are *his*. If we choose to fight in our own power or if we choose to abdicate the fight and pretend there is no battle, we lose. We have one hope—hide in the shepherd and allow him to wield his sword on our behalf. But if we wander away from him or try to take on the wolves on our own, we will be slaughtered.

The course of the battle changes when we stand on the high ground and fight with the weapons of our shepherd. Our imperfect love is completed in Christ, as his love fills us and flows through us into others. Knowing with certainty in our hearts how much Jesus loves us, not based on our human knowledge but based on revelation through the Holy Spirit, we no longer fall for the fearmongering tactics of the enemy.

We don't fear death because we know we are redeemed. We don't fear rejection because we know we are worth loving—not because of self-esteem, but because God loves us. Others' opinions no longer have power over us because we rely on Christ's truth to guide us. We no longer protect or defend ourselves because, in humility, we trust Jesus as our defender. His peace stands as a guard over our hearts and minds (Philippians 4:7), protecting us as well as warning us of any enemy's attacks.

In addition, Christ's salvation and his righteousness, through which we are sanctified, opposes and repels the condemnation and shame of the enemy (Philippians 3:9). While we are uncertain of our identity without Jesus, his truth shows us who he created us to be, and we can use the sword of his Spirit to go on the offensive against our enemy, challenging the sins of pride and rebuking all claims against our nature.

Our enemy looks for vulnerabilities, cracks through which he can sneak in his perverse words. These openings are places where we still hold onto control or where we doubt God's love and truth. When we believe and trust God, and act on our belief in humility and submission, the deceptions and accusations of the enemy begin to bounce off, finding no vulnerable ground on which to land. All the pieces of the full armor of God work together to block the enemy's access.

Do you see how little power the enemy actually has against us when we stand in Christ? In fact, because of Christ, the enemy can do nothing to us unless we permit him access by agreeing with his deceptions. When we center ourselves in Christ's truth, the enemy flees back into the darkness like a little rat who fears exposure in the light. When we focus on how much Jesus loves us, and we allow that love to flow into others, we push back the darkness and reclaim territory for the Kingdom. In these ways, love and truth overpower the enemy and overcome his lies.

While I'm sure all these things I'm describing sound good, you may be wondering how to access such power.

God gives us a foundation from which to live—the interweaving of his identity with our own. Our oneness with God is our true foundation. Without that foundation, we are a feather in a storm, unanchored, vulnerable, and tossed around at the whim of circumstances. So, let's explore how oneness with God provides our strong foundation, our anchor in the storm.

In the Vine

Let's revisit the parable of the vine and branches. The centerpiece of this parable is Jesus' admonition, "Remain in me, and I will remain in you" (John 15:4a). Whatever life flows through us flows from his Spirit, and whatever fruit we produce grows by his Spirit. In nature, a branch cannot live without the vine. If we don't remain in Jesus, our spirit slowly dies. I described the process of that slow death in the first section of this chapter. We begin as his perfect creation and end a battered shell. As Jesus described it, "If anyone does not remain in me, he is thrown out like a branch and dries up" (v. 15:6a).

But we must keep in mind, *this outcome is not God's will.* It is the natural consequence of separation from the vine, not something God desires or causes. Jesus' prayer tells us his will for us is to be one with him, just as he and the Father are one.

When we remain in the vine, our nature as part of the vine is made clear. We begin to see the aspects of the vine's nature in our own being. Our similarities to the vine—its covering and color and texture and structures—become apparent. No, we aren't as strong as the vine or as grounded, but we gather our strength from the vine's deep roots. As the vine nurtures us, we take on more and more of its characteristics.

The same is true when we remain in Christ and allow Christ to remain in us. We are strengthened by his strength, rooted and grounded in his love. The fruit of the outpouring of his Spirit grows from us. Our ability to trust returns as we see his trustworthiness, his consistency, and his follow-through on his promises. Our fear is cast away by his perfect love as we learn there is no punishment for those perfected in love. Our shame washes away as we learn there is no condemnation for those in Christ.

Any sense of being bad, unworthy, or unloved is banished by the deeply embedded experience of the height, depth, and breadth of his love for us. Our value is evidenced by his choice to go to the cross—for us. Our meaning and purpose are made clear as we partner with him to usher in his Kingdom. We begin to see ourselves through his eyes, recognizing the substance of aspects of his nature in us.

We stop relying on ourselves, so his strength becomes our strength, his security becomes our security, and his freedom becomes our freedom. We let go of judgment because we trust his righteousness. We no longer grasp after control—we don't need to because we trust him and know his goodness. And we relinquish our pride in exchange for humility, because we accept we are not God, and we know nothing.

We grow and breathe and live as long as we are connected to the vine. Our strength flows from his strength. Our spirit is one with his Spirit. Our identity is anchored on the firm foundation of who he is.

Reflecting His Nature

Living in this fallen world has consequences. The relentless destabilizing and obscuring of your God-given identity are some of the most serious consequences, leaving you with deep insecurity and doubt, and an insidious desire for control. As a result, you quickly lose sight of the aspects of your identity that reflect God's nature—which creates a profound sense of emptiness and loss, but you don't know why you feel empty or what you have lost.

So, how do you recover what you've lost? First, you need to understand the God-aspects of your identity aren't lost. They are only hidden from you. What God has woven into your identity cannot be destroyed. Even into eternity, those elements that make you who you are will still be there. Given that truth, the goal becomes to remove the coverings blocking those God-aspects from your vision and awareness.

This process begins with reconnecting to some aspect or aspects of your true identity. Try asking these questions in prayer to see what Jesus reveals to you about your nature and his nature expressed in you:

1. What are my earliest memories, and what do those memories show me about the ways I reflect God's nature?
2. What consistent positive patterns can I recognize in my life, and what do they reveal about my true identity?
3. What qualities of Christ's nature am I most drawn to?

These questions can be helpful guides for exploring your true nature with Jesus, but I encourage you to ask him how he wants to help you uncover your identity, then follow his lead. Be as open as possible to what he shows you or speaks to you.

The next part of the process involves partnering with Jesus to remove the coverings so you can reflect his nature fully. Identifying the sources and makeup of those coverings becomes the next objective. In prayer, ask these questions and see what Jesus provides as insight for you as you seek the sources:
1. What beliefs do I hold that are hindering my identity?
2. Where am I giving weight to my emotions over truth?
3. What tactics of the enemy can I recognize as effective against me, and what do those tactics tell me about where I am most vulnerable?

You start with your beliefs. Your objective is to take each hindering belief to Jesus, surrender that belief into his hands, and ask for his truth to replace the old belief. This process may be quite involved, as often false beliefs are bound to each other in a self-reinforcing pattern, so uncovering one lie may reveal two more. But the process remains the same—surrender into dependence, give the belief to Jesus, and ask to receive his truth in exchange.

You may also find you benefit from a prayer partner in this process, either a trusted spiritual mentor, a Christian counselor, or a friend with enough spiritual maturity, discernment, and insight to help you sort out the lies when they become entangled. But if you don't have anyone who fits this description, don't be dismayed. Jesus will show up for you and provide what you need to walk out this process with him.

If you don't know when beliefs are covering your identity and blocking its flow into the world, you can use certain feelings as signals or red flags warning you of the presence of lies. Feelings associated with the fruit of the Spirit, such as love, joy, and peace, are what I call green-flag feelings. They indicate the presence of truth. Our red-flag feelings include fear, shame and blame, doubt, bitterness, hopelessness, and pride, which shows up as self-judgment or judgment of others.

When feelings arise, accept your emotions, which means you acknowledge them as your feelings and accept responsibility for them. Then, you evaluate the feelings to see if they are based on truth or lie beliefs. Several options for evaluation of your feelings are open to you:

1. Compare the feeling with the fruits of the Spirit. If they don't match his fruit, they are lie-based.
2. Ask Jesus what belief produced that feeling, then ask him if the belief is true or false.
3. Listen to your inner dialogue—also known as self-talk—and see what self-talk preceded or is associated with your feelings. Then evaluate your self-talk to see if it is rational (based in reality and reason) or irrational (based in misperceptions, flawed thinking, or imaginings).
4. Look for key words in your language. Certain word choices are associated with lie-based feelings. For example, fear shows up in our language as have to, must, can't, and what if. Shame language includes should, ought to, and fault, whether directed toward yourself or others. Judgments—self-demeaning or self- aggrandizing statements—show up as not good enough, never measure up, don't matter, unloved, better than, more than, and all up to me. Recognizing these words can lead you to the lie.

Again, Jesus is your best resource here. Irrational emotions can seem rational when you're in the middle of them. Lies *feel* true when you believe them. So, you'll need his help to step out of the feeling and assess honestly and accurately. After you accept responsibility for your feeling, through prayer, present the emotion to Jesus and request his evaluation. He will be gentle, and you can trust his response.

You can know you're hearing from Jesus if his truth produces those green-flag feelings of peace, joy, love, hope, relief, lightness, and/or freedom in you. Even conviction from the Holy Spirit, which is different from condemnation, brings peace, relief, freedom, and hope. But if what you receive from prayer brings the red-flag feelings of shame, fear, worry, condemnation, blame, and/or debasement, you can know you've not heard from Jesus. What you heard may be your own judgment from the lies you believe, or from the enemy, who is quick to accuse.

If your feelings are based on truth, you embrace, express, and act on those feelings. If based on lies or irrational thinking, you halt any action based on the emotions and surrender the feeling to Jesus. Finally, you seek his help in choosing a different emotion based on a new, truth-based way of thinking.

For example, let's say I have just entered a room where a large group is gathering for a party. People are standing in clusters of various sizes, chatting. I walk up to one of the clusters, and no one acknowledges my presence. Instead, they continue their previous conversation. I feel hurt, embarrassed, and rejected. Those responses feel true to me, so I choose to leave the party.

If I followed the process as I've described it instead of walking out on the party, I would first acknowledge my hurt and shame and woundedness and admit to myself I have chosen these feelings. I then accept responsibility for my choices.

Evaluation comes next. Are those feelings rational? Did the group actually reject me or were they simply in mid-conversation? Plus, I didn't introduce myself or speak to them, either. Which is a more rational explanation for them not speaking—having never met me, they decide to hate and reject me, or they were already talking with people they already knew, and I didn't speak or introduce myself to them? Did I actually do anything wrong, which would lead to a sense of shame? Or is my shame based on my own lies of unworthiness? Did I knowingly commit any sin?

And/or I listen to my self-talk and look for the key words indicating lie beliefs. I find "I'm not wanted, I don't matter, I'm stupid, I'm shameful, I have to leave", and I recognize those beliefs are lies.

And/or I look for the fruit of the Spirit in my feelings. Am I feeling loving? Joyful? Peaceful? If not, the feelings are lie-based.

Now, I turn to Jesus. I confirm with him my evaluation. I find he often affirms me—though not the feelings—and comforts me in my woundedness, despite the irrationality of my beliefs. But along with his loving kindness and care, he will gently correct the beliefs behind my irrational emotions and remind me of truth. In this case, he might gently remind me the world doesn't revolve around me, which my assumption of their immediate dislike presumes.

He would likely confirm his love and acceptance, and that he will never reject me. If I know I'm loved and worth loving, the sting of others' actions doesn't strike home in my heart. As a result, I no longer assume they didn't speak because of something wrong with *me*. My emotions change from hurt to peace, and my actions change from leaving to waiting for a break in the conversation and introducing myself.

The final objective involves recognizing and learning how to combat the tactics of the enemy on a consistent basis. I've observed Satan takes the easiest road, so he exploits our preexisting vulnerabilities. But we can use his tactics against him. If we see the patterns, we can even discern our identity from what he is trying to undermine and how he's trying to cover it up.

I offer you a sampling of his tactics—and I do want to point out he isn't creative, so he tends to be repetitive and predictable—but his application with you will be tailor-made for your identity, so my samples are far from exhaustive.

With someone who is sensitive in their nature—like when Jesus is moved to deep compassion by someone's suffering or calls the little children into his arms—and the hurts of a fallen world come to them, the enemy will try to convince them to shut down their heart to avoid the pain, then whisper to them their disconnection from their heart protects them and helps them, when in reality it hurts them. Notice how shutting down their heart effectively closes off their sensitivity and natural compassion. Satan has, for all intents and purposes, rendered their identity null and void.

When someone has a strong-willed nature, perhaps someone created to stand against the enemy—like when Jesus stood on the steps of the Temple and called out the Pharisees or turned over the moneychangers' tables—Satan will accuse them of being harsh or offensive. He'll call being strong-willed names like hard-headed and stubborn. He'll try to convince them to despise their nature and try to put on a softer aspect, cutting their legs out from under them and leaving them weakened in the fight. Do you see how his lies leave them ineffective because they aren't living from their God-given identity?

Someone who is given a free spirit—like when Jesus walked across the water or spoke with the Samaritan woman at the well or encouraged his disciples to gather grain on the Sabbath—will likely be accused of being flighty, silly, reckless, or childish. Satan will try to steal their joy through any means open to him. He'll prompt parents, teachers, and friends to admonish them to take life more seriously and follow the rules. He'll tell them discipline is punishment for being who they are. Over time, they'll be shaped into clones, and the light they shine into the hearts of others will be snuffed out.

These are a mere sampling of the types of tactics Satan uses. Do you see patterns and similarities in the stories?

Once you identify the patterns, you can partner with Jesus to establish defenses against the enemy's tactics. Recognizing when the enemy uses fear and shame is a good first step, for fear breeds control and shame breeds judgment. As I said, fear language includes have to's, can't's, must's, and what if's. Shame language includes should's and ought's, as well as fault and blame statements. With

Christ's help, learn to listen to your inner dialogue, and interrupt the internal voice when you hear any of these words.

As Jesus reveals more truth to you, you can write down his truths to create a readily available reference for recall when you get tripped up by one of these tactics. I like to use images and songs to represent truth Jesus has shared with me. I surround myself with these images and listen to the appropriate songs when Satan attacks in familiar territory.

You can also plan with Jesus to develop strategies that work well for you. Keep in mind the Scriptural instruction to put on God's armor, and in everything, to *stand firm* (Ephesians 6:11-18). Do your days go better when you start the day in prayer? Do you fend off enemy attacks better when you read Scripture consistently? Does going over your truth list frequently help you to stay anchored? Does speaking with a spiritual partner help you stay grounded? Does having a heart of gratitude for the aspects of God's nature he knit into you fill your heart with love and help you resist enemy attacks? How about sharing the truths you've learned with others?

But be careful you don't turn these strategies into "have to's"—remember, that leads to fear-based thinking which leads to control. Instead, develop a number of strategies you can pull from that work for you, and choose to use one or more of them when you recognize an enemy assault.

What does any of this have to do with reflecting the nature of Jesus?

In the same way the enemy shuts down your identity using lies, Jesus frees your identity using truth. Once you have walked with him through the process of uncovering your God-given identity, you are free to begin living from that identity, allowing it to flow from you into others like the living water Christ described to the Samaritan woman. Without the shroud of lies in your way, not only can your nature flow freely, but you'll more readily hear from Jesus in prayer.

His Spirit lives in your heart, so when your heart is closed and covered, it's more difficult to connect to him and hear his voice—not impossible, just more difficult. But when the lies are lifted, your communication becomes continuous. You no longer have to stop and focus or sit for long periods of silence seeking a way through the morass of lies. As your connection grows, so does your trust and faith in his goodness.

Instead of trying to be like him because you "should" or "have to" to be acceptable to him, now you are assured you are always acceptable, always loved, and always valued. Now you *want* to be more like him since your love for him is growing and deepening. Those aspects of his nature woven into the deep places in your heart blossom in his light and spread like flowers in a fertile field.

Now, the leadership of the shepherd takes on new meaning. You no longer wait to look for Jesus during crisis to fix problems and rescue you. Instead, you walk with him all the time, sharing openly as he guides each step. Your relationship becomes less about outcomes and more about the process.

For example, I rarely ask Jesus for a specific outcome, not because I believe it's in error to do so, but because I trust the process of living life as his partner. I know that no matter what happens, he is with me in it and will walk me through it. My focus is on our relationship, not on the state of my immediate or future circumstances. Why would I need to be concerned about outcomes when I'm assured of his constant presence?

This world stops being my only reality. In fact, it fades into the distance, a backdrop for my relationship with Jesus. My spiritual reality—the Kingdom reality—overtakes my vision. I'm not blind to the world, I simply don't give it weight. The temporal loses importance in my eyes, while the eternal takes on a new magnitude of prominence. Therefore, those things that last into eternity—love, relationship, the expression of my identity, service to others, and the coming of his Kingdom—take on a gravity they didn't have before. These things consume my thoughts and inform my actions.

I understand I will never be fully like Christ until I reach the Kingdom. After all, my identity doesn't include all of his nature, only those aspects chosen by God for me to reflect. But the closer I hold to the vine, the more I start to look like the vine. And the more I grow, the more like the vine I become.

Questions

1. Where does your pride hinder your relationship with Christ and leave you vulnerable to the enemy?
2. Consider your own internal World War for a moment. What are some battles you have fought or continue to fight within yourself?
3. In what areas of your life do you need to align yourself with God and his ways?
4. What patterns do you recognize in how the enemy tries to attack your identity?
5. What aspects of God's identity do you recognize in your nature? How do you reflect his nature into the world?

Prayer

My Jesus, I love you. And I love the aspects of your nature you've chosen to share with me. I'm grateful for the gift and the trust you show me by sharing those qualities with me. Help me always keep those qualities in sight. As the fallen world and the enemy attempt to cover up my nature, strengthen me, Lord, to stand in my God-given identity. Keep me consciously aware of the tactics of the enemy and the lies I have chosen to believe. Shine your light of truth into my heart and sear away the shroud that covers me. Where my mind is divided, bring unity and wholeness. Where I am wounded, bring healing. As I remain connected to the vine, make me more like you. May your Spirit flow through me in a tangible and powerful way, and may I, as a result, allow your Spirit to flow into the world through me. In the holy and wonderful name of Jesus, Amen.

Donna E. Lane, Ph.D.

THE WILL OF THE SHEPHERD

"I am the resurrection and the life. The one who believes in me will live even if he dies, and the one who lives and believes in me will never die. Do you believe this?" (John 11:25-26).

What is God's will for our lives?

On the last night before his arrest, Jesus prayed for all believers, "…just as you, Father, are in me and I am in you. I pray that they will be in us…the glory you gave to me I have given to them, that they may be one just as we are one—I in them and you in me" (John 17:21a, 22-23a). What a deeply meaningful, beautiful prayer!

Jesus is asking God to create the same oneness in us that he shares with Jesus. He wants to be fully immersed in us, his Spirit flowing through all our cells and inhabiting our hearts and minds. In the same way, he wants us to be completely immersed in him, buried with him, and resurrected into a transformed life where we are one with him in every way.

From Philippians 2:5-11, we know Jesus is fully God who shared in the human nature. He experienced oneness with God while fully sharing humanness with us. Because he was willing to take on the human condition and fully experience it with us, we can also experience oneness with him—he in us and us in him. This was Jesus' prayer.

He desires to wash away the shroud of the fallen world, with all its insecurities, fear, and doubt, and restore us to our created identity. Through him, we are *born again*. We share in his resurrection. He wants those aspects of God's nature woven into us to shine from us and flow out into the world. And from the glory of his nature in us, he brings his Kingdom to this world.

Jesus calls himself the resurrection and the life. In our limited, temporal understanding, we may associate his words with the event of his resurrection, but Jesus is speaking here of his identity. He didn't say, "I will be resurrected." He said, "I *am* the resurrection." He didn't say, "I'm alive." He said, "I am *the* life." What is Jesus describing here?

To try to comprehend his statement, we must first consider his transcendent and eternal nature. Hebrews 13:8 tells us, "Jesus Christ is the same yesterday and today and forever!" Similarly, Malachi 3:6a (NIV) says, "I, the Lord, do not change" and Psalm 102:25-27 (NIV) states, "In the beginning you laid the foundations of the earth, and the heavens are the work of your hands. They will perish, but you remain; they will all wear out like a garment. Like clothing you will change them and they will be discarded. But you remain the same, and your years will never end."

Consider for a moment the implications of these statements. *Everything that God is, he has always been and always will be.* Therefore, all aspects of his nature and his experiences have been from the beginning and will be for all eternity.

We view Jesus' life through our temporal lens, beginning in the manger and ending at the ascension, because this is how we experience life—bound in time and lived in a linear progression with a start and a finish. But if we step out of the limitations of time for a moment and contemplate the nature of the eternal, we begin to understand his experience isn't limited. He *is* the beginning and the end, the Alpha and Omega, all at once.

This great mystery is described in John 1:1-3. "In the beginning was the Word, and the Word was with God, and the Word was fully God. The Word was with God in the beginning. All things were created by him, and apart from him not one thing was created that has been created." The Greek *Logos* translated as "Word" here means the transcendent eternal, the unchanging universal truth—in other words, the divine nature. The author of John uses the Greek *Logos* to refer to Jesus, emphasizing he *is* the divine nature.

Jesus has always been one with the Father. *He is One.* Given the prologue in John, we accept this as truth. What we don't often consider are the implications of the transcendent and eternal nature of Christ. *He is all.* He is not bound by time. He transcends time, which means he carries all his experiences eternally. He contains all within his being. He was, is, and always will be an infant, a child, a man, and divine. He is, has always been, and will always be resurrected.

And he is, has always been, and will always be one with us.

We also accept he made all things, but we don't consider that to make all things, he must contain all things. So, once again, Jesus *is* the child. He *is* the nature of a human. He *is* the resurrection.

And we are all found in him.

He is all in One.

As Paul writes, "yet, for us, there is one God, the Father, from whom are all things and for whom we live, and one Lord, Jesus Christ, through whom are all things and through whom we live" (I Corinthians 8:6). Since he created all things and through him all things live, his life is *the* life. He contains all.

As a Child

Jesus came to us as a child and instructs us to come to him as a child. Many sermons have centered on what he means by "become like little children" (Matthew 18:3), but I want to suggest a slightly different take on this verse. Recall I described how Jesus contains all of his experiences, unbound by time? Yes, Jesus came to us as a child, but he still is the child. What if the innocent child who is Jesus desires to be our playmate? What if he is saying he wants us to share in his joy? His freedom? His innocence?

What if sharing in his joy, freedom, and innocence *is* entering the Kingdom?

Humans have five basic needs: survival, love and belonging, authority, freedom, and *fun*. Since Jesus makes it clear he meets all our needs, wouldn't it make sense he would meet our need for fun as well? I think we often visualize Jesus as somber and serious—and to some degree, we are right to do so, since his mission in coming was a solemn task with genuine suffering involved. But we miss the playfulness and humor in Jesus—the childlikeness that *must* be there because he is the child—when we only focus on the seriousness of his task.

We don't diminish him when we see him in the total aspects of his human form. On the contrary, we enrich our view of him because in his humanness, he expresses the many dimensions of our nature, and we can relate to him more.

In a similar teaching, Jesus states we must be born from above (John 3:3) to enter God's Kingdom—not born, *reborn*—reborn into the identity he created at our inception, dead to all the influences and taint of the fallen world. We must be the child as he is the child.

Jesus resolved sin by his death, but he ushered in his Kingdom through his resurrection. In the same way, it is our being reborn that ushers in the Kingdom within us, for through our oneness with Christ and sharing in his resurrection we return to who he made us to be. Our spirit is joined with his Spirit, which frees us from our old ways of sin and the shroud of the world.

This oneness is a created, restorative work of the Holy Spirit. As Jesus said, "what is born of the flesh is flesh, and what is born of the Spirit is spirit" (v. 6). When we are one with Christ, we live centered in our spirit, one with God's Spirit—a spiritual being rather than a fleshly being. We can't see with our physical eyes the transformative work of the Holy Spirit, for it is done by his will and his presence alone (v. 8), but we can sense it in our spirits. As John 6:63 says, "The Spirit is the one who gives life; human nature is of no help! The words that I have spoken to you are spirit and are life" (the best translation of the Greek here is spirit-giving and life-giving).

But that's not all the Holy Spirit accomplishes. The wind—or Holy Spirit—blows wherever it wills. We see its impact in the movements and impressions and sounds it creates in the world, even though we don't know the source or destination (John 3:8). Again, Jesus emphasizes *we don't know*.

He blows through us which creates movement in the world in ways we can't understand. His movement through us changes others in ways we may never perceive. His Spirit united with our spirit pushes back against the presence of evil and reclaims territory from the enemy, but how he accomplishes this is beyond our infantile knowledge. And he does all this while we live freely in his presence, filled with all the things children enjoy—love and belonging, comfort, freedom, fearless abandon, security and safety, wonder, and most of all, joy—"an indescribable and glorious joy" (I Peter 1:8b).

Do you see in his words the importance of childlikeness? When we are open and unguarded, we are ready to share in the divine nature through the work of the Holy Spirit within us. We must be restored to how our created nature was at our beginning, and we must be reborn in the Holy Spirit and made one with Christ for this to be accomplished. When all the aspects of God's nature he created within us are resurrected like Ezekiel's valley of bones, where the wind/Spirit of God breathed life into death, just as God told Ezekiel he would accomplish, we are purified and given a new heart and new spirit, removing the heart of stone, and restoring a living, breathing heart reflecting the Spirit of God.

That new, childlike heart joins with Jesus to share in his joy and freedom and innocence. Our eyes are opened to see God's creation anew, with wonder and awe instead of apathy or disdain. We feel Christ's love filling us and receive it freely and openly, without question or doubt, like a child receives her best friend with joy and bounds into shared play with abandon.

What is the nature of our play with Jesus? If you have children, you understand imaginative play is the most fun. God created us this way, in his image, with the ability to imagine and create. In other words, we are co-creators with God. He has willed to share his authority with us and to partner with us in creating his story. What an amazing gift! What an incredible play partner!

Think of our play like a toddler finger painting. We make huge messes and mix up all the paint, and our clumsy fingers can only make smears on the paper, but Jesus can take what we create and make it into a thing of beauty. Even our mistakes become works of art through his redemption of them. And after we're finished, he is there to clean up our messes.

In this way, Jesus meets us as our fun and creative playmate but also as our good parent, for all children need both love and instruction. He is able to share his childlikeness and at the same time be our Father, because he is all in One. And while we tend toward chaos and destruction, he brings order and peace to our chaos, and restoration and redemption to our destruction.

The shroud of the fallen world tends to suppress our imagination and creativity, which in turn limits our shared experience with God. As we lose our childlikeness and become more focused on worldly things, we become distant and disconnected from God. Our partnership in creation wanes, and instead we become a destructive force. We exchange our joy for worldly pleasures or accomplishments, our free spirit for the illusion of control, and our imagination for the concrete and tangible world of our senses.

Paul warns of the enticements of earthly accomplishments and fleshly pleasures. "If someone thinks he has good reasons to put confidence in human credentials, I have more. But these assets I have come to regard as liabilities because of Christ. More than that, I now regard all things as liabilities compared to the far greater value of knowing Christ Jesus my Lord, for whom I have suffered the loss of all things—that I may gain Christ and be found in him" (Philippians 3:4, 7-9a). When we seek satisfaction in the pleasures of the world and exult in the things we believe we've accomplished, those things are where we put our confidence. In fact, those things become our faith. Thus, Paul warns and instructs us to view those things as liabilities and count them as loss.

What does Paul mean when he writes to, "gain Christ and be found in him"? To gain Christ is to receive him into ourselves, wholly and completely; in other words, to allow Christ to fill us with his Spirit and unite with us as one. To be found in Christ is to immerse ourselves in him, to give away ourselves, and unite as one in him. This process is the fulfillment of Jesus' prayer in John 17:22-23— "that they may be one just as we are one—I in them and you in me."

Until children are trained by the adults in their lives to measure themselves by the outcomes they produce, children delight in the process of creation itself. Much like the attitude of God in Genesis 1, they look at their smeared paint and proclaim it good simply because they enjoyed creating it. They build with blocks for the sake of building and tear it down without regret so they can build again. They dance for the joy of dancing, not for the applause. They imagine themselves to be tigers or pirates or puppies or unicorns and revel in the fun even though this imaginative play produces nothing tangible.

Is it possible for us to return to this state of mind?

Not only is it possible in Jesus, he called us to do so.

Adulting

Hold on a minute, you're probably saying. We can't spend our whole lives playing! We have responsibilities. Jobs to go to. Families to provide for.

True.

Jesus also had responsibilities, serious things he came here to accomplish. Within him is the adult, alongside the child and the parent. But I believe Jesus calls us to maintain a childlike *state of mind,* where we do not worry about what we will eat or drink or what we will wear, where we don't worry about what will happen tomorrow but focus only on today, where we seek joy in all our endeavors, and where we make the process of living more important than the outcomes we produce.

None of these attitudes preclude handling our responsibilities or doing our jobs. They do require shifting our focus off of results and changing our priorities from external rewards or acknowledgements to relationships and joy.

So, what would good adulting look like to Jesus?

Jesus is clear he desires for us to have an abundant life (John 10:10b). He doesn't promise material abundance—in fact, he indicates material wealth often produces spiritual difficulty—but he brings with him a rich, full life overflowing with joy, love, reverence, and an appreciation for beauty in all its forms. These qualities produce a spiritual abundance that transcends the worldly, mundane existence. For Jesus, a transcendent life is an abundant life.

Since Jesus said he came for us to have this abundant life, how does he provide it?

He gives us himself.

The first ingredient of an abundant life is the presence of Jesus within us. True abundance cannot be built from any other foundation. Along with his presence, Jesus adds the richness of our nature, those elements that make us who we are, into the mortar for our foundation. Like mixing ingredients to make concrete, he folds the complex, multifaceted elements of his nature into the characteristics he wove into our nature until they are inextricably bound and solid as a rock. On this foundation, he builds an abundant life.

And like concrete, the fewer impurities or extraneous elements are present, the stronger and more resilient the foundation.

As he joins his identity with ours and we immerse ourselves in him, our point of view begins to change. The appeal of the superficial enticements of the world—transient fleshly gratifications, counterfeits of joy like approval, praise, and other external awards, mind-altering chemicals, a false sense of safety, the feeling of superiority or power over others, and all the flashy, glittery, trendy fads that catch our eyes and draw us in—those things fade like old, washed-out black-and-white photos, becoming flat, indistinct, and undesirable.

In their place, Jesus enlivens our desire to live from our spirit and allow our true nature to flow freely into the world. Jesus then fills our hearts with love. Truly knowing the full extent of his love and having his love fill us to overflowing equips us to love well. His love flows through our hearts and out into others without hindrance because we already know we are loved. His love allows us to love who he made us to be, which then opens our hearts to love those around us, as he instructed when he told us to love our neighbors as ourselves (Matthew 22:39).

Our self-expression no longer focuses on striving to achieve status or power since we recognize the intrinsic value of our identity. Our goal becomes to live according to our God-given identity in everything we do, whether it be work or play or relationships with family and friends. Living from our true nature in union with Jesus is why we are here—he made us for that purpose and positioned us in time and place to fulfill what only our natures can fulfill in the coming of his Kingdom.

Choosing the loving action becomes our heart's desire. We allow Jesus to show us what is the loving thing to do in every circumstance. With his help, and through the overflow of his love within us, we express love into the world, pushing back against the darkness and furthering his Kingdom.

In addition, we begin to express our God-given authority over our choices, beliefs, and feelings. As a result, we stop blaming others for our problems. When we're hurt by others' actions, we evaluate ourselves and our response to find what caused their action to hurt us—specifically, what lie belief their behavior stirred in us, because we realize no one has the power to hurt us unless we allow it through some belief *we* hold. Once we recognize our lie and seek truth from Jesus, we're able to readily forgive their misbehavior.

We also stop taking responsibility for the feelings and actions of others or expecting others to take responsibility for ours. Because we recognize our own authority, we begin to recognize each individual's personal authority over their own choices, beliefs, and feelings.

So, when others say, "You made me feel…" we don't fall into the trap of trying to "control" their feelings or "fix" things for them. Instead, we take care of our own actions and feelings. We continuously check with Jesus to see if we have made any choices out of alignment with him and our true nature. If so, we decide to choose differently next time. But we do not take responsibility for the feelings others have chosen, or the actions others have taken.

And when we choose poorly, we no longer shame ourselves. Instead, we take responsibility for our actions through repentance and making new choices, because we recognize both the forgiveness of Jesus and our own authority to learn from our mistakes and choose differently in the future.

We no longer let our fleshly feelings determine the choices we make. Remember, we have authority over our feelings, authority given to us by God. Instead, we identify consequences—both positive and negative ones—from our choices before we make them, then choose actions which best align with Christ and match our true nature to produce the consequences we desire.

We also know we have the authority to choose our feelings. We do so by altering our beliefs to produce the feelings we choose. For example, if I make a mistake, I can choose to believe I'm a failure, or I can choose to believe I can learn from the mistake and grow as a result. Do you see how each belief produces a very different feeling?

In this mindset, feedback from others loses its power. Now, I know most of us like the feeling we get when we receive positive feedback—negative feedback, not so much. But we don't recognize the pitfalls of giving power to any feedback—even positive feedback. Internalizing feedback opens us up to reliance on external sources for validation of our identity, and we don't want any source beyond Jesus to have power there. Only Jesus knows our true nature in its fullness, so only he can give us genuine and accurate feedback. All other feedback is personal opinion based on limited human perception.

That doesn't mean feedback has no value. Listening to input from others, taking that input to Jesus for evaluation to see if anything good for our growth can be found there, and receiving the helpful information through Christ can be of great value.

For example, if my husband tells me I was selfish in a particular decision I made, I choose to not internalize that feedback—which leads to shame or defensiveness, because his input speaks to my identity, not to my choice. Instead, I go to Jesus in prayer and ask him if I was indeed selfish. Jesus will help clarify for me if I could've made a more *loving choice,* effectively separating my action from my identity, and focusing instead on love. If so, I can make a different choice from a place of peace and certainty, free from shame or condemnation, with my identity intact.

In the same way, if my husband tells me I'm brilliant, I don't internalize that feedback either—which leads to pride and self-aggrandizement, because once again, his input speaks to my identity and gives me a false sense of accomplishment. Instead, I go to Jesus in prayer and ask him for input. He gives me a heart of gratitude for his many gifts and keeps me grounded in the truth with humility. After all, anything I know, I know because he has told me.

Finally, Jesus girds us with truth. His truth secures all of his other weapons of spiritual warfare and prepares us to fend off worldly encroachments and enemy attacks. Truth becomes like soap for our souls, providing a daily—hourly—minute-by-minute cleansing from anything from the world or the enemy that tries to "stick" on us and worm its way into our hearts like a spiritual cancer eating away at our identities.

What I'm describing is freedom—true freedom from the influence and power of the external world. Our citizenship is in heaven (Philippians 3:20). As a result, we are aliens in this world—invading soldiers from another realm seeking to overthrow the powers and principalities of this world. We can't fight against what we are accepting as a part of us or agreeing to internalize. Remember, we can't fight on both sides in a war.

The Kingdom mindset helps us externalize this world and transcend it. We anchor ourselves in our identity merged with Christ into one. We are filled with his love which flows freely, along with our identity, into this world. And we are secured with God's truth.

Our worldly desires shed like dead skin. Judgment evaporates, replaced by personal authority, choice, and responsibility. Striving transforms into *being*. The shackles of others' opinions fall away. We live and breathe and move as one with Christ in his realm within us and allow all that he's created in us to flow out into the world.

As Paul described, "Now those who belong to Christ have crucified the flesh with its passions and desires. If we live by the Spirit, let us also behave in accordance with the Spirit" (Galatians 5:24). The Holy Spirit and the shroud of the world have opposing desires, so we can't live by both. If we are one with Christ, we live as he lived. We do as we see him doing. We follow his guidance as our shepherd. We are "transformed by the renewing" of our minds (Romans 12:2b), not receiving the spirit of the world but receiving the Spirit who is from God (I Corinthians 2:12).

Oneness with Jesus lived out in love and truth is adulting, according to Christ. Any other foundation is wood, hay, and straw, revealed for what it is in the fires of suffering and trial where it burns up and leaves us anchorless, drifting and alone (I Corinthians 3:12-13). But through his presence, we're able to remain grounded in the truth of who he is and who we are, made whole by Christ and made one with Christ. Our identity and love flow out into the world instead of the things of the world flowing into us, allowing us to transcend the world and experience his Kingdom now.

Equipped

Have you even heard someone say, "God won't give you more than you can bear"? I've heard this statement from Christians, quoted as if it is a Scripture verse.

It isn't.

As our enemy often does, two sections of Scripture have been taken out of context—remember how Satan tempted Jesus in the wilderness?—and twisted into this oft-quoted saying. So, let's take a look at these verses and see what the Bible is really telling us about God's equipping.

The first is found in I Corinthians 10:12-13 (NIV)—"So, if you think you are standing firm, be careful that you don't fall! No temptation has overtaken you except what is common to mankind. And God is faithful; he will not let you be tempted beyond what you can bear. But when you are tempted, he will also provide a way out so that you can endure it."

The verses in I Corinthians begin with the admonishment to be careful and not complacent. Standing firm takes intentionality, focus, and perseverance. Just before this verse, Paul describes the failings of the Israelites as examples of how easy it is to be deceived, even though they had witnessed the miraculous. He then states the temptations we experience are nothing out of the ordinary or uncommon to all—so no excuses there.

Now, the next section is the one so often misquoted. Paul opens with God's faithfulness. He has placed limits on the extent of temptation at Satan's disposal, and those temptations are common to everyone. Note the verse says, "no temptation." The Greek word translated temptation here, *peirasmos*, is the same word used to describe the temptations of Jesus in the wilderness. The literal Greek refers to something revealing weakness in you. The literal translation of "beyond what you can bear" is "beyond what you are able." In other words, you are able to withstand the temptations common to mankind. So, no temptation exists beyond your ability to resist.

Then, Paul tells us how we endure temptations. God provides us with a "way out"—meaning he offers us a path other than the path of falling into temptation. Think of it as standing at a fork in the road. Jesus gives us a choice that leads away from temptation, while the enemy offers us another path, one in which we agree to go along with the enemy—*but it is our choice.*

A paraphrase of this section might go something like this— "Don't get complacent—be vigilant so you don't fall. We all have to deal with the same temptations, but God's faithfulness means you are able to withstand those temptations we all face. God gives you a choice—take his path or choose the enemy's path. This makes any temptation manageable."

In these verses, Paul isn't referencing the life circumstances that cause us pain and suffering. We don't choose those. I know I've gone through circumstances I never would've been able to handle without God's presence in the midst of them. Paul is specifically referring to something that is our choice—the temptations of the enemy—where it's up to us to choose, yes or no. God has equipped us, so we are able to make the choice to follow his path. But, as Paul warns, we must be careful not to get complacent, or we could choose poorly.

The second verses are from Hebrews 13:20-21—"Now may the God of peace who by the blood of the eternal covenant brought back from the dead the great shepherd of the sheep, our Lord Jesus, equip you with every good thing to do his will, working in us what is pleasing before him through Jesus Christ, to whom be glory forever."

The Hebrews verses speak of doing God's will. The prayer of the author of Hebrews is for God to equip us with "every good thing" to do his will. Of course, it remains our choice to do his will—or not—but once again, he equips us so it's not beyond us to make that choice. It is through Jesus we are equipped. These verses echo the I Corinthians verses regarding God's faithfulness and provision.

Prepared

In addition to equipping us, God prepares us. According to II Corinthians 5:1-5, he has prepared us to be clothed in our heavenly dwelling, so that "what is mortal may be swallowed up by life" (v. 4b). The Holy Spirit has been given as a guarantee of sorts, a deposit or pledge or down payment on our Kingdom dwelling, ensuring our preparation by bringing his Kingdom to reside within us.

Through the Holy Spirit, we have taken off "the old" and "have been clothed with the new" (Colossians 3:9b-10a), just as Christ described in John 3:3-6 when he said we must be born from above, born of spirit so we may be spirit. Christ prepares us, according to our willingness for him to do so, by crucifying our flesh (Galatians 5:24), along with all our worldly desires. This preparation—this spiritual rebirth so we may live clothed in the Kingdom—is accomplished by the Holy Spirit in us, not by our effort. No amount of behavioral effort will birth me of the Spirit or clothe me with the new.

So, we circle all the way back now to rebirth and coming to Jesus as a little child. How does an infant enter the world? They are *totally dependent.* In order to survive, they must attach to their parent or caregiver, for they can't provide for their own basic needs. Through this attachment, the child remains an extension of the parent. Ideally, this attachment is secure, based on the responsiveness and love of the caregiver, and trust grows in the child.

Then, by God's design, the child begins a process called individuation. They begin to see themselves as a separate being, with their own identity. Again, under ideal conditions, the parent supports their exploration and development of independence and encourages the expression of their God-given nature. Through this process, the child begins to discover who they are and realize their authority to choose.

Again, according to God's design, as the child grows in their knowledge of who they are, they choose to shift their attachment to God. They return to dependence, coming to Jesus as a little child, but with an important difference. They are no longer attached for survival—their attachment is based in faith and love. As God reveals their identity in its fullness, he empowers them to express their nature into the world. At the same time, without threatening the individual's unique identity, Christ provides the opportunity for oneness with him—and they are clothed in Christ.

This process is how God prepares us to be "clothed in our heavenly dwelling." I've described here the ideal process as God designed it to work. But this is a fallen world, and things are less than ideal. Parents are fallen people raised by fallen people, so no one pulls it off perfectly.

Sometimes the child believes they must remain an extension of their parent, due to the parent's insecurity or desire for control and the child's coexisting desire for value and worth. When this type of attachment occurs, the child's discovery of their identity is thwarted. The child's attachment becomes insecure and anxious, and their relationships remain need-based instead of love-based.

The insecurity turns into a set of beliefs about themselves, including such beliefs as they are unloved, they don't matter, they are unworthy, they aren't good enough, or they don't measure up. They tend to use relationships to give them their value and worth. I think you can see how these beliefs become hindrances in the development of oneness with Jesus. Instead of joining with Jesus in love, they seek Jesus based on need. They focus their attention on what Jesus can do for them or give them instead of on the relationship.

Sometimes the child's basic needs are not met by the parents, or the parents are unpredictable. Another possibility is inconsistent or permissive parenting. The child doesn't develop basic trust in these scenarios and forms a fearful or avoidant attachment, which can lead to beliefs such as it's all up to me, I have to do it myself, I'm alone, and even a sense of entitlement or narcissism. Can you see how these beliefs would hinder oneness with Christ? Why would I turn to Jesus if I have to do it myself? Why would I trust Jesus if I've never trusted anyone but myself?

Suffice it to say, as parents, we have many ways to get it wrong.

The good news is, even in the midst of our flawed attachments and imperfect individuations, God prepares us to "take off the old" and become "clothed with the new." The imperfect attachment with the parents is replaced with a secure attachment to God, who loves and parents perfectly. The old beliefs are shed like dirty clothes and are replaced with God's truth. The distorted identity, based on the imperfect mirrors available to us in the world, is swept away, revealing the true nature created by God, which has been hidden underneath the piles of debris from the world.

Through this process, God redeems his original design, and we are reborn—like a little child—and made new. Our dependence shifts to God, who knows and revels in our true identity. Through his presence in us, we are made ready for our heavenly dwelling.

God's Will

So, according to Hebrews 13:20-21, we are equipped with every good thing to do God's will, and according to II Corinthians 5:1-5, we are prepared to be clothed in our heavenly dwelling.

But what is God's will? And what is meant by our heavenly dwelling?

According to the Hebrews verses, as we join with our great shepherd, we are equipped with all the good things we need—Jesus in us, and we in him. This is the work Jesus is doing in us. God sees us as one, as Jesus and he are one, and he is pleased. From this position of strength, our God-created identity, joined with Christ, flows into the world, pushing back the forces of evil and reestablishing a foothold for his Kingdom here, as we wait for his coming to create the new heaven and new earth.

The II Corinthians verses contrast our earthly bodies with our spiritual dwelling place and describe the deep desire we feel to be clothed in our eternal dwelling. In other words, Paul is expressing our desperate need for the Kingdom. We groan inwardly for the heavenly dwelling now. We crave to be swallowed up by life.

But we must realize our eternity doesn't start when we die. It begins when we receive Christ, along with the Holy Spirit as our guarantee. So, through the Holy Spirit and the process of rebirth, God prepares us to live in the Kingdom right here and right now.

As we join with our great shepherd, we are prepared for his purpose, which is to live as one with him in the Kingdom. Our "earthly tent"—meaning the ways of our flesh—are dismantled, and by the work of his hands we are clothed with our heavenly home. Through his Spirit, we experience the Kingdom of God within us, and his Kingdom flows from us into the world in power, standing against the tide of evil as we anticipate his Kingdom coming in fullness.

This is God's will for us—through rebirth, for our true nature to be immersed and made one with Christ and for us to be clothed in his Kingdom now. The power and presence of his spirit in us enables our genuine identity to flow freely into those around us. His equipping and preparation strengthen us to stand firm against the enemy, regaining territory lost to the evil one and ushering in his Kingdom.

Yes, we are meant to prepare the way for his coming.

Questions
1. What comes to mind as you consider Jesus containing all things in his person—a child, a man, a mother, the cross, the resurrection—and most of all, what comes to mind when you consider he contains *you*?
2. I Peter 1:8 talks about belief in Jesus producing "an indescribable and glorious joy." In what ways do you experience this kind of joy—the unrestrained freedom and fun in the heart of a child?
3. What kind of counterfeit, transient "impurities" does Jesus need to cleanse from your foundation through immersion in his Spirit?
4. What enemy enticements and temptations common to all are you most vulnerable to? How has Jesus equipped you to choose to transcend them?
5. In what ways has Jesus prepared you for your heavenly dwelling?

Prayer
Precious, wonderful Jesus, you are all to me. I so desire to immerse myself in you, and for you to fill me completely with your presence so you may purify my heart. Please birth me anew in your image, as a child in spirit and freedom, and as an adult in wisdom and truth. Free my heart from its restraints so I may have fun with you, Jesus. Take away my self-consciousness and help me to be only conscious of you. Equip me with what I need to be able to choose wisely and continue in innocence as I face the enemy and the corruption of this world. Prepare

me to live in the Kingdom of God from this day and for all eternity. Lord, may I truly be one with you in all my ways. Above all, I choose you. Amen.

SHEPHERD

SURROUNDED BY WOLVES

"I am sending you out like sheep surrounded by wolves, so be wise as serpent and innocent as doves" (Matthew 10:16).

Preparing the way for Christ's return is a dangerous business.

Jesus said he was sending the disciples out "like sheep surrounded by wolves." Along with this statement came an instruction: "so be wise as serpents and innocent as doves." This verse begins a long narrative where Jesus describes what the disciples will face because of their beliefs. Their future includes being arrested, tried, beaten, killed, and hated even by members of their own family because of the name of Jesus. Yet, he instructs them to shout what they've heard and seen from the rooftops.

The question that arises for me is why a *good* shepherd would send his sheep into the midst of their greatest enemies?

Before we can explore this question, we need to understand Jesus' instruction. First, we've already seen how Jesus identifies us as the sheep of his pasture who know the shepherd and recognize his voice. We've also read how Jesus identifies himself as the good shepherd who would die to defend his sheep. In this verse, Jesus continues the metaphor, but with a twist.

The Jewish people already saw themselves as sheep surrounded by Roman "wolves." In Jewish culture of the time, wolves represented violence and destruction—for example, imagery in I Enoch, an ancient Hebrew apocalyptic text, describes Israel as sheep who invited slaughter and were therefore handed over to wolves and other wild beasts to be devoured. But instead of being handed over to be devoured, Jesus equips his sheep with the words they are to say, the wisdom to deal with their persecution, and the innocence to transcend it.

So, Jesus is willing to send his sheep out among the wolves because he resides in us, and we reside in him (I John 2:27). *We never go it alone.* As we saw in the previous chapter, the "great shepherd of the sheep" equips us with everything we need for all he calls us to do (Hebrews 13:20-21). And we see in the responses of the apostles the strength of Christ as they faced their wolves willingly and without fear.

Stephen—stoned to death for testifying before the High Priest and the Council—saw heaven open and witnessed Jesus standing at the right hand of God in the midst of the stoning (Acts 7:54-60).

James—sentenced to death by sword for testifying before Herod—according to tradition, as he testified, his guard was so moved he confessed Christianity, and the two were taken away and beheaded together (Acts 12:1-2).

Peter—imprisoned in chains (Acts 12:1-11), crucified upside down—by tradition, because he felt he was unworthy of being crucified like Christ (John 21:18-19).

Andrew—bound on an X-shaped cross until he died after preaching across Asia—by tradition, continued preaching for the three days he was on the cross (Acts of Andrew, Book of Martyrs).

Philip—crucified upside down after converting a proconsul's wife—by tradition, he preached from the cross and the moved crowd asked for him to be released, but he asked to remain on the cross and that they free Bartholomew instead (Acts of Philip).

James, the brother of Jesus—pushed from the pinnacle of the temple where he was preaching—by tradition, then he was beaten with a fuller's club and stoned to death (church records).

Simon the Zealot and Jude—hewn by an axe after commanding demons to come out of idols and destroy their own images—by tradition, even though it was clear weather, lightning hit the temple three times the same hour they died (Golden Legend).

Antipas—when commanded in Pergamum to renounce Christ and make a sacrifice to idols, refused—by tradition, locked inside a flaming hot copper bull, where he prayed forgiveness for his tormentors, then went to the Lord peacefully as if he simply fell asleep (Revelation 2:12-13, church documents).

Paul—kidnapped (Acts 21:27), beaten (Acts 21:30-31, 23:3), arrested (Acts 21:33, 22:24, 22:31, 23:35, 28:16), shipwrecked (Acts 27:41), bitten by a viper (Acts 28:3)—and never stopped preaching and writing until, by tradition, he was beheaded by Nero (Clement of Rome).

What gave these men and countless other martyrs the strength to continue to tell others about Christ in the face of stoning, crucifixion, beatings, imprisonment, beheadings, burning, and lions in the arena? The supernatural peace recorded in so many of these stories, despite unimaginable pain, indicates the Holy Spirit's power was at work.

Jesus warned his disciples with exactly what would happen and promised the Holy Spirit would provide what they needed at the time. Look at his specificity and detail as he prepares them.

> "You will be handed over to councils and beaten in the synagogues. You will stand before governors and kings because of me, as a witness to them. First the gospel must be preached to all nations. When they arrest you and hand you over for trial, do not worry about what to speak. But say whatever is given you at that time, for it is not you speaking, but the Holy Spirit. You will be hated by everyone

because of my name. But the one who endures to the end will be saved" (Mark 13:9b-11, 13).

Without the indwelling Holy Spirit, I don't believe anyone could've endured. And without the words of the Holy Spirit, I doubt Christianity would've survived the disciples' generation.

Do we take Christ's warning seriously? When the promised trials come, will we truly be ready to stand? Is our connection with Jesus strong enough to receive the words we must say in the moment we are to say them? Can we withstand being hated by everyone because of the name of Jesus?

Are we prepared?

Serpents

For the Jewish people, serpents were seen symbolically as cunning and shrewd. Some believe Jesus is instructing his disciples to use the same cunning and shrewdness as the enemy to defeat the enemy, without losing their dove-like innocence. I don't see it that way. I don't believe Jesus intended for us to use human wisdom or evil's tactics to fight evil.

The same Greek word translated in Matthew 10:16 as *wise* is used by Jesus in the parable of the ten virgins, referring to the wise virgins who made sure to bring enough oil for their lamps. Those five virgins prepared. They thought through all eventualities, including the possible delay of the bridegroom in coming. They equipped themselves for the task.

Oil carries tremendous significance in Scripture and is often associated with the presence of God's Spirit. Oil was used to anoint kings and consecrate them as holy to the Lord. For example, when the Lord identified David as his chosen king over Israel, he told Samuel to anoint him with oil. According to Scripture, "The Spirit of the Lord rushed upon David from that day onward" (I Samuel 16:13b).

If the oil for the virgins' lamps represents the Holy Spirit, Jesus is instructing us through the parable to prepare for what is to come by being filled with his indwelling Spirit. The oil for their lamps provided light in the darkness of night. The foolish virgins weren't prepared and sought to take the oil of the wise virgins, those who were ready and filled with the Spirit. But we can't borrow from someone else's relationship with Jesus. Oneness with Christ is an individual and personal experience.

So, I believe Jesus is instructing the disciples—and us—to prepare well for the journey, to thoughtfully consider what we are taking on and what it will mean for us, and to make sure we are equipped with all we need to finish the assignment. In other verses, Jesus warns the disciples to count the cost of being a disciple (Luke 14:26-32). I see him doing the same thing in this verse.

The same Greek word is also used by Paul when he talks about not being wise in our own knowledge or conceited, but to be wise in Christ (Romans 11:25, 12:16, I Corinthians 4:10). In our oneness with Christ, we are not to rely on our own wisdom. We can't depend on our knowledge or understanding to navigate any circumstance. We are to put our faith in Christ's wisdom, follow his guidance each step, and trust him to walk with us through the outcomes, whatever those turn out to be.

In the case of the disciples, the outcomes were as Jesus described—arrest, trial, imprisonment, beatings, and death. If they relied on their own wisdom, do you see how they would've never embarked on the journey? Human cunning puts survival above all else. A shrewd person would've slunk away into the darkness, never to be heard from again.

Jesus uses the analogy of the "wise" serpent to emphasize the disciples' need for *his* wisdom to be equipped for what he knows lies ahead. He isn't pointing toward human cunning or Satan-like shrewdness as methods for us to use during times of trial. "For the wisdom of this age is foolishness with God" (I Corinthians 3:19a).

Scripture never mentions growing in human wisdom, but repeatedly admonishes us to grow in spiritual wisdom—the wisdom of God.

Return for a moment to the discussion about Jesus carrying all experiences within him, unbound by time. Jesus knew exactly what his disciples would need to walk their path of suffering because Jesus had already walked the same path and would always walk the same path. "Jesus Christ is the same yesterday and today and forever!" (Hebrews 13:8). Having walked the path, Jesus is able to show us the way. The path exists within him, and he lives within us.

The author of Ecclesiastes makes some interesting points about human wisdom. First, he observes oppression turns a person with human wisdom into a fool (v. 7:7). In other words, human wisdom doesn't stand in the face of adversity. When he tried to examine the nature of life using human wisdom, he found it was beyond human understanding and deeper than can be fathomed (v. 7:24). And when he tried to gain human wisdom to understand God and all that he does on earth, he discovered he couldn't grasp or comprehend any of it (v. 8:16).

When Paul preached about Jesus, he says he didn't speak with "persuasive words of wisdom" but with the Spirit's power "so that your faith would not be based on human wisdom but on the power of God" (I Corinthians 2:4-5). Because of our inherently limited knowledge, distorted perceptions, and shroud of the fallen world, relying on human wisdom is folly. Human wisdom will always fail.

But God's wisdom contains all, just as God contains all. He created wisdom; therefore, he *is* wisdom. When we receive wisdom from God through his presence within us, we are able to face the wolves and stand strong as the apostles stood, continuing in peace despite suffering and speaking only the words we receive from his Spirit.

The five wise virgins were prepared for the Bridegroom's coming. They had invested their time and resources toward filling themselves with his Spirit instead of investing in other, worldly things that gave momentary pleasure or transient reward. When the darkness came, the time for using their oil, they had what they needed.

Are we like the wise virgins or the foolish virgins? Do we believe we have it "under control"? Do we delude ourselves that we have enough oil for our lamps to remain in the light during the deepest darkness? Or do we invest our time and resources into our relationship with Christ? Are we humble enough to realize we cannot and will not stand without his presence filling us, creating oneness with him?

Doves

In Jewish culture, doves were symbols of purity and integrity. They were also seen as harmless creatures, so oblivious to danger they remained innocent of its ways. I believe here Jesus is pointing back to maintaining our childlikeness, even in the face of great suffering. To never cause harm, to keep our integrity, to remain pure despite circumstances—these are Jesus' instructions.

Human nature seeks to return harm for harm. Even the Jewish law proclaimed, "an eye for an eye" (Leviticus 24:20). But Jesus instructs us to remain pure and innocent of evil responses, while still responding according to God's wisdom.

Note Jesus is not telling the disciples to lie down and roll over here. He instructs them, if they are persecuted in one town, to flee to another. He also tells them wherever they are not received to shake the dust from their shoes and leave. He urges them to speak with the words the Holy Spirit gives them to say, and not use their own words. He encourages them not to fear their persecutors and reminds them their persecutors can only kill their bodies but can do nothing to their spirits.

Fundamentally, he is telling them to be the five wise virgins, who were not passive at all but were instead well-prepared and ready for their calling. He cleanses us and sanctifies us, so we are reborn, and our God-given identity is released from bondage. He lifts the shroud from our hearts. He transforms us into his likeness by renewing our minds. He digs out the lies planted deep in us and replaces them with truth. He provides what we need to maintain our purity and integrity in the face of the world's embrace of evil through the presence and power of his Spirit. And by his Spirit we reflect his Spirit—the dove—into the world.

Readiness

Speaking in the context of signs of the coming of the Son of Man, Jesus warned his disciples:

> "But be on your guard so that your hearts are not weighed down with dissipation and drunkenness and the worries of this life, and that day close down upon you suddenly like a trap. For it will overtake all who live on the face of the whole earth. But stay alert at all times, praying that you may have strength to escape all these things that must happen, and to stand before the Son of Man" (Luke 21:34-36).

While this text refers to the time of Christ's return, the warning is relevant to every day of our lives. We don't know the day or hour of his coming, so we must always be ready. In addition, our wolves are always on the prowl, looking for ways to catch us unaware. We can't ever afford to be complacent. We must be ready.

The Greek translated here as "be on your guard" is literally "watch out for yourselves"—

> Watch out for getting weighed down with worry.
> Watch out for what overtakes your time and attention.
> Watch out for what absorbs your mind.
> Watch out for what captivates your heart.
> Watch out for self-indulgence.
> Watch out for being consumed with day-to-day life such that you miss what really matters—the things that are eternal.

His warning is prompting us to realize how easy it is to be distracted and consumed by worldly circumstances and tempted by our fleshly desires. Any day could be "the day" when adversity strikes us. If we are not intentional in keeping our focus on Jesus and fostering our continuous connection with him, "the day" will "close down upon (us) suddenly like a trap." Hardship and suffering can take our legs out from under us—and quickly.

My youngest son was 18 months old when he first evidenced the symptoms of eye and hand tremors. Eight years and multiple doctors later, we finally had a diagnosis—albeit one of those general neurological diagnoses that means "in the family of inflammatory disorders" like ALS or MS—but no real treatment options. A series of trial-and-error treatments failed to stop the progression. Four years later, and he is intubated for the first time when he stopped breathing in his sleep. And three years later, he was home with Jesus.

I can honestly say, if I had not already developed a deep, intimate connection with Jesus, these circumstances would've leveled me. And I'm not sure if during these events I would've had the wherewithal or ability to build that kind of relationship with him, were it not already in place.

My "day" came upon me and lasted fifteen-and-a-half years. As Jesus said, you never know the day or the hour. But because I was ready, and I walked in oneness with Christ with my eyes focused on the eternal and not on the temporal circumstances, Christ strengthened me to stand throughout my son's illness and death.

Yes, many days were incredibly painful, but Jesus walked through them with me and gave me great peace and joy in the midst of the pain. His death was crushing, but I received Jesus' comfort in my mourning. My grief continues to this day—and will until the day I approach the gates of heaven and see Jesus with Cody by his side to greet me—but as my sweet son said, "It's only an interim."

Jesus offers two more instructions in these verses—stay alert at all times and pray. The original text translated as "stay alert" means to be *sleepless*, which is an interesting—and enlightening—choice of words for Jesus to use. To remain alert means to stay watchful, vigilant, and wide awake—refer back to the ten virgins parable. If at "the day" of great trial, we aren't ready and have to try to purchase oil for our lamps, because of the distractions of our emotions and the pain of those times, Jesus warns we will have difficulty "making it back in time" to be with the Bridegroom.

To stay alert also means being quick to notice and recognize potential danger—refer back to Jesus' directive to be as wise as a serpent and innocent as a dove. We must develop the skills of identifying wolf attacks at their onset and recognizing our vulnerabilities *before* our "day" arrives. We must practice intentionality in keeping our eyes fixed on Jesus *before* the need for his strength arises. Our ability to stand on that day depends on it.

Jesus describes two areas of focus for our prayers—praying for strength to escape the circumstances and praying for strength to stand before the Son of Man. Again, while these prayers are referring to the time of Christ's return, they are also relevant to any times of difficulty.

When Jesus says strength to escape, I don't believe he means to avoid them. That interpretation makes no sense in context, because he has just indicated that what must happen will "overtake all who live on the face of the whole earth." We aren't going to avoid the trials of the end times any more than we can avoid suffering in our lives. Plus, why would we need strength to escape if escape means to avoid? Avoiding is the easier road.

I believe his suggested prayer is to escape being overtaken or destroyed by the trials. Certainly, times of suffering take great strength to make it through, and our strength alone is not enough. Praying for his strength to endure with your faith intact and escape the devastation of your spirit in the process would be an appropriate and beneficial prayer.

Praying for strength to stand, both during trials and when you come face-to-face with Jesus to hear what he has to say about your life, are also valuable prayers. Our strength alone won't avail us during the relentless presence of our wolves when we're walking through adversity. You see, they recognize, often better than we do, how exposed and susceptible to deception we can be when exhausted by enduring hardship. Remember, wolves attack vulnerabilities, and do so in force. We need Jesus' strength to stand up against their assaults.

In the United States, I'm not sure we take Jesus' instructions in this section of Scripture to heart. Our lives have been comparatively easy for some time. The thought of people "fainting from fear" over the signs in the heavens and on the earth and the "powers of heaven" shaking with wrath and vengeance doesn't make it into our everyday conversation. And since the church has not known widespread persecution in America for generations, I believe we've become lackadaisical in our preparedness. We seem to have forgotten the dangers of being the five foolish virgins who do not have enough oil for their lamps.

Notice in the parable that both the wise and the foolish virgins fall asleep when the Bridegroom is delayed. This reminds me of the three disciples who fell asleep while Jesus travailed at Gethsemane. No matter how deeply we love Jesus and want to be with him, our "spirit is willing but the flesh is weak" (Matthew 26:41). We, too, seem to have fallen asleep, which is the very thing he warned against.

Do we actually believe Jesus' warning? Do we think we are exempt because we live in a supposedly free country? Are we relying on our participation in church to provide our oil when the time of trial or persecution comes? Have we invested ourselves in deepening our personal relationship with Jesus, such that his presence fills us so fully, we know what he is saying without stopping to ask?

The fruit in today's church says to me we are not ready.

It's as if the church has fallen into two widely divergent extremes. Both accept Jesus Christ as savior, but one maintains a close tie to the laws of the Old Testament which fosters judgment and condemnation and exclusion in their people. Rules, not love, and sin, not grace, tends to be their main focus of conversation. These churches foster a works-based mentality more than a Spirit-led relationship. An example of one expression of this extreme is so-called Christian nationalism. Does love flow freely from these churches? Does the world experience the presence and power of the Spirit in their actions?

The second camp leans to the other extreme—a kind of anything-goes mentality which removes both depth and discipline from a relationship with Jesus. For them, the church becomes a feel-good place where they are uplifted but rarely challenged, where they are entertained but rarely transformed. It's pleasant to go to these churches. The social relationships developed in small groups are beneficial and fun. But does the church experience translate into a deep abiding in Christ? Do members demonstrate the fruit of his presence and God's wisdom in their daily lives?

Neither extreme lives out the truth of Christ.

In this breach, the church has become vulnerable. No wonder churches are bleeding people, particularly younger generations. Where is the transformational power of the Holy Spirit? Where is Christ's love on full display in all its glory? When I talk to young people who have left the church, I routinely here the word, "irrelevant." How has the church become irrelevant in their eyes? They often say the church has nothing of substance. They point out the hypocrisy and judgment and want nothing to do with either.

The Holy Spirit has the power to restore our true identity and to fully integrate our nature with Christ's nature until we are one. He has the power to help us transcend the struggles and sufferings of this world and live on a higher, more meaningful plane where we know we are loved and valued and are able to love and value others well. He is able to give us a peace beyond any "peace" we can find through human means—a peace that isn't transient or temporary but sustains us throughout any circumstance. And he is able to bring us into the fullness of an abundant life overflowing with joy, love, beauty, and reverence.

Why don't these people who are leaving the church in droves experience all of these phenomenal—and *powerful*—gifts?

Perhaps the church, in its lack of preparedness, no longer teaches or evidences these qualities. Maybe the church as a whole is asleep. We need to ask ourselves, if we were the ones spreading the gospel to all nations for the first time, would anyone listen? If we walked up to Simon and said follow me, what in us would compel him to follow?

What will happen to the church when times of adversity come—for they come to all—or when the persecutors return—for they will. Jesus is clear we will all be hated for what we believe because he was hated when he was physically present here. We may be experiencing the birth pangs of persecution now, with the widespread social criticism of the church going on in our country at this time. But these critiques are nothing compared to what the disciples/apostles experienced—and what Christians in other countries experience this very hour.

If we are to stand when suffering and persecution come, we must return to the transcendent and transformational power of a deep oneness with Jesus Christ. We must allow the good shepherd to actually lead us in every moment of our lives. We can no longer settle for seeing Jesus as we might see the local pastor—someone we seek out on occasion to ask a question or receive a lesson—or the local grocer—someone we go to when we need something from him—or the local police officer—someone we turn to when we're wronged for him to fix the problem.

We've become so used to being independent and self-reliant, we've forgotten the depth of our need. At the same time, as a nation, we've never been more depressed, more anxious, more traumatized, or more self-destructive than we are at this time. We don't need easy, pat answers or a fix for our problems. We need *so much more.*

We need to feel seen. We need to be heard. We need open-armed embrace. We need the kind of love that doesn't settle for us staying in the same predicaments we've known or accept our creating the same destruction for ourselves we have in the past—a love that sees beyond the shroud to our true selves but won't allow the shroud to continue its hold on us.

We need to know how much we are loved like a child knows they are loved when their parents provide structure and consistency and loving discipline. We also need support and encouragement on our journey, where we're allowed to express ourselves, explore, and take risks, so we can learn and grow.

We need to be challenged in our complacency. We need to be motivated to move beyond our comfort. We need a power beyond our own strength, wisdom beyond our own limited knowledge, insight beyond our ability to see, and authority beyond our weakness in the face of our wolves.

Our Wolves

While I've been making the case that suffering and persecution are coming for us, that isn't to say we don't face wolves, right here and right now, every day of our lives. On the contrary, our wolves are alive and well, and very much active in their attempts to steal, kill, and destroy.

Perhaps our wolves are more crafty and cunning than we realize. Rather than coming at us in a full-frontal assault, using swords and crosses and lions, our wolves take more subtle approaches. Maybe they use camouflage to disguise their presence and intention, like the big bad wolf in Little Red Riding Hood. Or they go underground and sneak into unknown crevasses and cracks in our foundation, hidden until they spread like cancer into all areas of our lives.

We need God's wisdom and truth to recognize our wolves, to make us aware of our vulnerabilities and blind spots, and to help us wake up from our complacent slumber.

Each one of us has individualized vulnerabilities, places in our hearts where the wolves planted seeds of lies. The enemy's overarching goal is to cover up our God-given identity, to render it useless for the Kingdom. Since our identities are unique, his tactics are designed for our specific natures. However, his approaches have certain commonalities. Remember, the enemy is not creative. Creativity is an aspect of God's nature, not Satan's.

I've talked about the lies of control and fear, shame and judgment, and the root of pride from Eden that we can be like God, *knowing* good and evil. These lies are common to all of us, and everyone believes some form of these lies.

Our wolves also seek to limit our choices and steal our freedom. When our choices are restricted, our freedom is lost, and when our freedom is lost, we cannot give or receive love, for love must be freely given and freely accepted, or it is not love. Do you see why our wolves would be invested in leeching love out of the world?

God *is* love. Because God has chosen partnership with us, he works through us to evidence his love and pour it into the world. By squeezing love out of us, the enemy limits God who otherwise has no limits. At the same time, the enemy can easily challenge our belief that God is good and loving, since we struggle to receive his love from a place of bondage.

Our wolves whisper all the things we can't do, all the things we have to do, and all the things we should do as ways to restrict our choices. Some common examples are I *have to* remain at a job I hate or in a relationship that is destructive to me; I *can't* take any risks because I might fail; I *should* be doing more work for the church or I'm not a "good" Christian; I *have to* take care of everyone else's needs because I'm selfish if I tend to my needs; I *can't* ever relax because something bad is going to happen; I *shouldn't* feel like I matter or am valuable to God because it's prideful to think that way.

Do you see the seeds of fear, control, judgment, and shame in these beliefs? The wolves' seeds grow into ensnaring vines, restricting our movements. They shut us off, shut us up, and shut us down.

I believe our wolves also influence us to seek comfort—not peace or joy, *comfort*. They entice us with the familiar and easy. They beguile us with the illusion of safety. Most of those familiar, easy, or "safe" ways are destructive to us. Many of those responses are ones we learned in childhood, so they are immature and lack God's wisdom.

A few examples are not saying no when we need to say no for fear of rejection, avoiding conflict through deference, making choices to gain approval from others, following the lead of our feelings, accepting mistreatment from others, defensiveness during confrontation, avoiding responsibility, setting no boundaries or inappropriate boundaries, indulging the cravings of our flesh, and other, similar responses. If we value comfort over peace and joy, these choices look appealing to us.

Scripture tells us the easy path is the road to destruction (Matthew 7:13-14). We are often faced with the choice between short term gain/long term pain vs. short term pain/long term gain. The easy choice is to go with short term gain because it delays the inevitable pain, not weighing the truth that the long-term pain is much worse and lasts longer when it comes.

Delaying gratification is the difficult path that leads to life, but few choose it because human nature doesn't like to deny itself. Our wolves cheer on and justify this aspect of the human condition. As a result, we have obesity, drug addiction, alcoholism, pornography addiction, sexual exploitation, child exploitation and abuse, idolatry in many forms, and the like—gratifications of the flesh that ultimately leave us the opposite of comfortable.

Our wolves also try to persuade us to avoid taking responsibility for our actions. They relish it when we play the victim. Yes, it's difficult to accept responsibility. Absolutely, it's easier to play the victim instead of looking within and doing the hard work with Jesus of changing our beliefs and feelings toward healing our hearts. But if we want to stand strong amongst the wolves, we must be wise—equipped and prepared.

Now, our society has jumped on board the victim train by promoting the belief that everyone has a justification for their state of misery, and it's always something or someone else's fault. We "can't help" doing hurtful or self-destructive things because of this reason or that experience. Even our popular language reflects a belief in the victim role, as our focus is on how others "made us feel" by their words, and how our feelings are now "triggered" by *something*—as if we don't have a choice about how we're going to feel.

Now, please understand me. I'm not saying trauma isn't devastating—quite the opposite. I personally know the terrible consequences of traumatic experiences. I also know all of us have endured or will endure some form of trauma in our lifetimes—for at the very least, all of us come into contact with death at some point.

But when you label everything as a trauma—for example, someone uses a word you don't like, someone expresses their beliefs around you and you don't appreciate them doing so, or someone disagrees with your point of view on a subject—you diminish those individuals who have experienced actual trauma.

Trauma is defined as an emotional response to a terrible or terrifying event like an accident, crime, or natural disaster. Hurt feelings do not rise to the level of trauma and are certainly not considered abnormal or extreme. Labeling hurt feelings as trauma doesn't remove responsibility for your feelings, beliefs, and actions.

We are all equipped by Christ to take responsibility for our feelings, beliefs, and actions because he has given us the authority to do so, and he has given us his presence to strengthen us in our weakness. Even during and in the aftermath of trauma, Christ is present with us to process those feelings with him toward healing.

Think of our responses to trauma as the emotional equivalent to physical shock. Some normal emotional responses to trauma include emotional numbing; hypervigilance—being always on guard and never able to relax; loss of hope; dissociation—a sense of being disconnected from yourself and your body; anxiety and depression; and emotional dysregulation—a sense of losing control over your anger, sadness, fear, and shame. All of these reactions are normal responses to abnormal or extreme circumstances.

Reminders of past trauma can stir up feelings in the present, but trauma doesn't supersede our ability to choose what we are going to do with those feelings. We are still able to recognize our responses are coming from our trauma, accept our feelings, and evaluate them with Christ for their validity in the here and now. Our feelings from trauma responses are still *our* feelings. They don't wield power over us beyond Christ's strength.

Our free will—the freedom to choose our beliefs, actions, and feelings—is ordained by God and cannot be abolished. The wolves try to convince us that other people's actions—including those which cause trauma—have the power to determine our feelings and responses. The wolves want us to feel like victims. We are not victims, just like Jesus never responded as a victim when he was tortured unlawfully. He recognized his ability to choose remained intact. As he said, "No one takes (my life) from me, but I lay it down of my own free will" (John 10:18a).

No one except God has that kind of power over me, and I don't want to give them that kind of power in my life in exchange for avoiding responsibility for my own feelings and actions. I choose to claim the authority Christ gave me over my feelings, beliefs, thoughts, and actions and exercise it fully. In doing so, I am reflecting the attitude of Christ.

Yes, at times during traumatic experiences, others may try to control your body through force—but they can never take away your ability to choose your feelings and beliefs, even if you are held down with a gun against your head. Corrie Ten Boom's story is a good example of this truth. Despite grave risk to themselves, Corrie and her sister chose to follow their hearts and hide Jews from the Nazis, until they were imprisoned and then sent to concentration camps. Even then, they continued to lead Bible studies and remained at peace within. Before she died in the camp, Corrie's sister famously said, "There is no pit so deep that He is not deeper still."

Perhaps the most important truth to remember is, no matter what your experience was, trauma doesn't determine who you are. What happens to you does not define you. God is the one—and the only one—who determines your identity. So, if your identity in Christ remains solid and secure, and your freedom to choose remains in place, what gives past trauma power in your present?

The answer to this question points us back to beliefs. With the exception of grief, which is a response based in truth, past trauma exerts power through the lies we come to believe about ourselves, about God, or about life due to the trauma. Those lie beliefs are based on our interpretations of the trauma. Even after the trauma is long past, the lies can continue to cause us pain in the present.

Some of the most damaging lies resulting from trauma are it's my fault—as if I am to blame for the trauma; I don't matter; God abandoned me or did this to me; I should've done something; I'm powerless; something bad is always going to happen; I have to protect myself; I'm tainted or damaged or broken; no one will love me—including God. This is not an exhaustive list, but it gives you a sense of the types of lie beliefs that can arise from traumatic experience.

Even grief, a normal and healthy response to loss, can be attacked by our wolves. Lies can creep into our thinking as we process our grief, such as, I didn't do enough for them; it's my fault; I should've told them I loved them more; I wasn't a good enough son/daughter/friend/parent, and other similar lie beliefs.

When we invite God to bring truth to these lie beliefs, God can change those beliefs by replacing them with truth. When the beliefs change, it changes our feelings, and the power of the trauma begins to lose its grip.

Remember, we all believe lies of some kind. Do you recall the discussion on how lies get embedded deep within us in our early childhood due to the fallen nature of the world in which we live? In their craftiness, our wolves try to match those early, deep-seated lies to the ways we interpret our trauma experiences. As a result, both sets of lies are reinforced. Often, they are repeatedly reinforced, and we reach what I call a light switch moment, where we fully accept the lie as absolute truth, and we turn out the light, never to examine or question the belief again.

When this happens, the lies become stronger, like a chain with intertwined links. You might've heard the word, "stronghold" used to describe when someone experiences a problem they can't seem to overcome. A simple definition for a spiritual stronghold is an interacting set of lies, perhaps arising from a generational sin, strengthened by repeated reinforcement.

I think of the story of the boy brought to the disciples who was made mute by a demon, but where they had succeeded before, this time they failed to cast out the spirit. When his father brought him to Jesus, and he cast it out, the boy suffered convulsions and looked so much like a corpse everyone thought he was dead. But Jesus lifted him up, and he was fine. When the disciples asked why they had failed, Jesus replied, "This kind can only come out by prayer" (Mark 9:17-29).

Prayer is our greatest weapon against our wolves. But we must understand what prayer is in order to know how to wield our most powerful weapon.

Prayer

We often think of prayer as presenting our requests to God or interceding on behalf of others. While these are important aspects of prayer, they don't present the primary function of prayer, which is to build connection and relationship with God.

We also tend to view prayer as a one-way communication, but Scripture describes prayer as both sharing and listening. According to Jesus, "My sheep listen to my voice, and I know them, and they follow me" (John 10:27). He also says, "The one who belongs to God listens and responds to God's words. You don't listen and respond, because you don't belong to God" (John 8:47).

Through our prayer, Jesus can speak his truth into our hearts to replace the lie beliefs we hold in our hearts. He can guide our steps and direct our path. He can warn us when wolves are at our door and help us stand in strength against them. And, of greatest significance, he can show us and tell us about himself and teach us about ourselves, including revealing who he created us to be. In prayer, we can receive our new name, the one he gives us to reflect our nature.

While the listening aspect of prayer can be a struggle at first, while our lies still shroud us and hinder our hearing, it's worth it to keep up the practice. Don't allow your wolves to tell you it'll never work or interpret the difficulty as meaning Jesus doesn't want to speak with you. Trust me, he always wants to speak with you, and he always has something to say. Remind yourself of the shroud—we all have lie beliefs—take a break for a few minutes and try again.

Once you perceive his voice—which can come to you in many forms—you'll begin to learn how to recognize his voice from the internal noise we all experience. Jesus offers this encouragement—his sheep follow him because they recognize his voice (John 10:4).

I've found three keys to discerning the voice of God:

1. The presence of peace
   In God's presence, we feel peace, and when we hear his voice, peace accompanies it. Even if his words are discipline or difficult truths, you'll know it's him because his peace settles over you as you receive what he has to say. By the same token, if what you hear causes anxiety, fear, distress, or shame, you are not hearing his voice but the howl of your wolves.
2. Agreement with Scripture
   Jesus only speaks what he hears God saying, so anything from Jesus will be in agreement with Scripture and Scriptural principles. If what you hear is contrary to Scripture, you are not hearing his voice.
3. Transformation
   Isaiah 55:11-12a states, "my word that goes out from my mouth...It will not return to me empty but will accomplish what I desire and achieve the purpose for which I sent it. You will go out in joy and be led forth in peace." In other words, nothing God says is wasted. What he speaks to you will produce the fruit of change in you. The change may be small, or it may be significant, but you will be transformed by his words. If nothing changes as a result of listening to Jesus, you are not hearing his voice.

When you hear God's voice, these three elements will be present. You can use them to screen out extraneous voices, such as your own voice or the voice of your wolves, and fine tune your ability to hear from God in the process. The more you converse with God, the more connected you feel to him, and the more connected you become, the closer you are to the oneness with Christ you desire.

One with Christ

Now, we circle back to the question at the beginning of the chapter—why would a good shepherd send his sheep out among wolves?

Paul wrote, "My aim is to know him, to experience the power of his resurrection, to share in his sufferings, and to be like him in his death, and so, somehow, to attain to the resurrection from the dead" (Philippians 3:10-11). What does he mean by "share in his sufferings"? And why would this be his desire?

First, it's important to note the overarching goal—to know Christ. At its core, this is the essence of the Christian faith. Certainly, knowing Christ means more than learning about him. Beyond that, I contend knowing Christ means oneness with him in all things. In the same way Christ contains all, including all aspects of our natures, we want to "contain" Christ such that he is fully one with us and we are fully one with him. We want to become so immersed in him that we become like him.

Paul was so completely invested in knowing Christ, he desired to share in everything Christ experienced—the power of the resurrection, his sufferings, and his death. He embraced his imprisonment and persecutions and beatings because Christ experienced the same. He wanted to know the resurrection from the dead because Christ had experienced its power.

Paul understood how Christ defined eternal life—"Now this is eternal life—that they know you, the only true God, and Jesus Christ, whom you sent" (John 17:3). In this prayer, Jesus is not referring to life after death but an eternal life*style,* a way of living that comes from a relationship with Christ. He defines this lifestyle as knowing God, not in the sense of knowing about God—in other words, not as human knowledge—but by experiencing God through relationship with Christ.

Peter also expressed the benefit of knowing Christ through sharing in his sufferings:

> "Dear friends, do not be astonished that a trial by fire is occurring among you, as though something strange were happening to you. But rejoice in the degree that you have shared in the sufferings of Christ, so that when his glory is revealed you may also rejoice and be glad. If you are insulted for the name of Christ, you are blessed, because the Spirit of glory, who is the Spirit of God, rests on you" (I Peter 4:12-14).

Like Paul, Peter understood how Jesus defined eternal life, and he viewed sharing in Christ's sufferings as something to rejoice about because they revealed his glory. He also saw persecution for the name of Jesus as a blessing because the Spirit rests on those who are one with Christ.

When Jesus came to earth, he walked among the wolves. Once he prepared and equipped the disciples, he sent them out among the wolves with his authority, and after his resurrection he sent them out again, filled with the presence of the Holy Spirit.

He sends us out in the same way—equipped with his power and authority, prepared with his truth, and filled with his presence. We are always with our shepherd. Through our shared experiences, we become more connected to him. The more he cleanses us of the shroud, heals our wounds, and replaces our lies, the more immersed we are in him, and the more one with him we grow to be.

The end goal is to become so completely connected with him, we know how he would walk at all times, and to be so immersed in him, we feel as he feels. This is true oneness.

We may live in a wolves' den, but our shepherd is mighty. He can defeat a giant with a slingshot and a single stone. He can shut the mouths of lions. He can rain down fire from heaven on his enemies. He can raise the dead by calling their name. When he is for us, who can stand against us? What do we have to fear?

Jesus is willing to send us out as sheep among wolves because he doesn't fear the wolves. He knows the wolves have no power over him. They are a vanquished foe. As long as he is in us, the wolves are held at bay. And when we are one with Christ, the wolves lose all power in our lives as well.

Questions

1. In what ways do you employ wisdom like the five wise virgins and maintain innocence like Christ in the wilderness in your dealings with the world and the enemy?
2. What vulnerabilities or blind spots do you need Jesus to bring to your awareness?
3. Which items on the watch list do you need to make a priority, so you are ready to stand against your wolves?
4. What lies have your wolves used against you? In what ways have the wolves tried to cover up your true identity?
5. In what ways do you know Christ? What do you feel about knowing Christ's sufferings as well as the power of his resurrection?

Prayer

Gracious Father, thank you for your presence and the opportunity you've given me to become one with you. Give me your wisdom, your strength, and your innocence as I walk among the wolves of this world. Help me to recognize and identify the tactics of my wolves, my areas of vulnerability, and my lies. As you fill me with your Spirit, bring forth my identity from behind the shroud of the enemy. As I seek your voice, make it clear to me so I experience more and more of who you are. Challenge me in my complacency to wake up and to stand. Bring me into full knowledge of the eternal lifestyle, such that our oneness is fulfilled. I praise you, Jesus, for your great love that makes all of these things possible. In your blessed name I pray. Amen.

THE SHEPHERD'S GIFTS

"All generous giving and every perfect gift is from above, coming down from the Father of lights, with whom there is no variation or the slightest hint of change" (James 1:17).

God's giving is a continuous stream, an unending outpouring from his heart of love for us.

From the tiniest moment of joy in a brief glimpse of beauty to the inestimable gift of his image as a part of our identity, God showers us with gift upon gift upon gift through every moment of our lives. But how many of his gifts do we miss? Our lack of awareness, tendency toward distraction, idolatry, and general blindness can hinder us receiving the gifts he pours out for us.

Our beliefs about ourselves can also interfere with recognizing the gifts he intends to give us, especially if we judge ourselves unworthy to receive good things from him. For example, his perpetual presence within us is his most glorious gift, but doubt or fear can cause us to close our eyes to his presence. We might assume he is judging us in the same way we judge ourselves. Perhaps we perceive his presence as transient and unreliable, and we must "find" him when we run into hardship. Or maybe we believe he is disappointed or inaccessible due to our unworthiness.

Our childhood experiences with our earthly fathers can have a profound impact on how we perceive God and receive his gifts. If we had a controlling, harsh father, we may assume God is the same, withholding when we don't measure up—which is basically never. A distant, uninvolved father can cause us to miss God's gifts because we're not looking for them. With a conditional father, we often experience God's love as transactional, a quid-pro-quo economy, where he gives us gifts *if* we perform certain services for him.

But can you visualize Jesus with arms folded, clucking his tongue and wagging his finger, saying I'll have something for you if you ever manage to get it right?

I hope not. Because Scripture certainly doesn't portray Jesus in that light, and the cross tells a very different story.

God is the righteous judge. He sees us through the lens of Christ's redeeming blood, not through the lens of our behaviors—or should I say, misbehaviors. When we receive Christ in our hearts and become one with him, we are "clothed" in Christ (Galatians 3:27). The love God pours out on us is the same love he has for Jesus, for we are fellow heirs with Christ (Romans 8:17). We are God's sons and daughters, no longer slaves. And like a loving father, he desires to share all his good gifts with us.

His gifts take many forms and means of expression. They can be tangible, physical gifts, internal, experiential gifts, and metaphysical or supernatural gifts. They can be momentary, to be experienced in the here-and-now, and they can be eternal. However, all his gifts have these things in common—they connect us to his Kingdom, they are for our good, they are given freely and without expectations attached, and we must look beyond the worldly with spiritually focused eyes to glean everything he has to offer.

When we allow our physical senses to dominate our perceptions, we tend to get bogged down in worldly experiences, missing the vast spiritual realm and everything happening there. Not only that, we lose sight of the spiritual connection all elements of this world contain. So, our perceptions become dulled and flat. The light of his Spirit inhabiting all things is dimmed to us.

I remember the first time Jesus opened my eyes to the spiritual realm. The biggest surprise for me was how it changed my experience of this world. It reminded me of the difference between picture tube television and HD TV. There was no comparison. Colors became brighter and richer. Dimensions were more pronounced. Edges were cleaner, sharper, and details were more vivid. The taste of food changed, too. What was once bland, nondescript sustenance became rich and savory fare.

Beauty became more than something pleasing to the eye—it became a full-bodied experience of connection with God. While walking on the sand listening to the roar of the ocean, I experienced the thunder of God's power and the soothing rhythms of his breath. Standing atop our ridgeline overlooking row after row of rolling blue mountains, I sensed the fullness of God's majesty as the trees carried the wind's continuous song of praise. Gazing into the night sky, I touched the edges of the vastness of God and recognized my infinitesimal presence under the stars. In the midst of such glory, the swell of realization hits me—he wanted *me*—and I'm overwhelmed with humility and awe.

Deep, abiding joy overrode momentary pleasure. Unshakeable and incomprehensible peace settled over my heart and mind, even in the midst of tragedy, loss, and hardship. His truth crushed the lies I believed about myself, about God, and about life, and planted new seeds of understanding which, over time, blossomed into new wisdom and understanding.

These are the gifts of God.

The Greatest Gift

When asked what God's greatest gift is, the instinctive answer is our salvation. But I wonder—how meaningful would our salvation be to us if not for his presence? From my perspective, the best definition of hell is separation from God. Salvation doesn't necessarily mean we experience his ongoing presence. Isn't that what nominal Christians do? They accept salvation but don't live out the relationship. So, to me, salvation is an empty, even self-centered word without the lived presence of God.

That's why I believe the greatest gift God gives us is his presence.

Keep in mind, God could've dropped us off and gone on about his business, leaving us to our own devices. This is the story told about most other "gods." Instead, he created us for relationship. Before we needed salvation, he walked side-by-side with Adam and Eve. His presence preceded salvation as his first gift.

When they created division through their shame with their free will choice to pursue knowledge, believing the enemy's lies that their created beings were not "enough", they chose to pursue being their own gods over love and life. Yet, God continued to pursue relationship with them.

And he continued his pursuit, calling us back to him each time we wandered away, over and over again, until finally, he stopped calling through the division and breached the gap himself, coming for us to reclaim us and restore us to relationship with him.

The fact of our salvation doesn't bring us his everlasting peace. Like most other facts, we learn it and move on to the next thing that grabs our attention. It is his presence which enables us to truly follow the shepherd. And in his presence, we find peace.

The rest of God's gifts flow from his presence. As I described, how we perceive the ocean, mountains, and sky, from the broad expanse of space to the tiniest flower, gains new dimension, substance, and meaning from seeing through his eyes. Authority, freedom, joy, truth, wisdom, and love all originate with him. In short, we have nothing without his gifting it to us.

So, what does his presence provide?

According to II Peter 1:3-4a, "his divine power has bestowed on us everything necessary for life and godliness through the rich knowledge of the one who called us by his own glory and excellence. Through these things he has bestowed on us his precious and most magnificent promises, so that by means of what was promised you may become partakers of the divine nature."

Breaking these verses down, we see his presence provides:
- Everything we need for life
- Everything we need for godliness
- The fulfillment of his promises
- Receiving his nature.

What do we need for life? First and foremost, we need salvation into eternal life, for our worldly life is fleeting, gone like a wisp of smoke in the breeze. To receive eternal life, we need the blood of Christ to cover our sins, and we need adoption as his children, to be "grafted in" to the vine.

We also need his provision. Do you recall the list of five basic human needs? They are survival, love and belonging, authority, freedom, and fun. Scripture speaks to each of these basic needs and God's provision. Jesus tells us we don't need to worry about our survival, including what we'll eat, drink, and wear, for God provides for the flowers and the birds, and we are more valuable to him than they are (Matthew 6:25-34).

Jesus himself provides us a place to belong and abundant love. He shares his authority with us, as he did with his disciples when he sent them out to make disciples of all nations (Matthew 28:18-19). In addition, his gift of free will affords us authority over our own actions, feelings, and thoughts. His death and resurrection provided for our freedom such that we are no longer slaves to sin or the law (Galatians 5:1). And I talked in a previous chapter about his provision for our fun as we come to him as little children in the joy and freedom of play.

All our basic needs are met in him.

What about what we need for godliness? He provides the Holy Spirit to lead us into all truth (John 16:13). He acts as our parent and our teacher, disciplining us when needed (I Corinthians 11:31-32) and instructing us in the ways of the Kingdom through his parables. He provides wisdom to those who ask for it (James 1:5), he delivers us from evil and temptation (Matthew 6:13), and he gives us all we need for the renewing of our minds so we can be transformed into his likeness (Romans 12:2, II Corinthians 3:18).

What about his promises? We see the fulfillment of his promises from his first covenant with Noah to his covenant with Abraham to his promises to deliver his people from Egypt and the covenant of the law to the coming of Messiah as prophesied in Scripture. Throughout, he has proven faithful to fulfill what he promises.

Through Christ's coming, he fulfilled his promises of redemption and restoration. He made it possible for us to be his people, as he is our God. Through our connection with him, he strengthens us, he lifts us up, and he provides for our rest. He answers us when we call on him, and he never leaves us or forsakes us. He is faithful and just to forgive our sins. He makes our pathways straight, fights with us in our battles, and delivers us from the evil one. These are a few of his promises which we see fulfilled in our lives on a daily basis.

In addition, we have promises to look forward to. He has gone before us to prepare a place for us, and he promises to return for us. We have an inheritance in heaven waiting for us. We will see the new heaven and the new earth, and at the end, we will sit with him on his throne.

Finally, we are indeed "partakers of the divine nature," for not only has he knit aspects of his nature into our created identity and made us in his image, he also lives within us and becomes one with us when we receive him in faith. He lavishes on us the richness of his grace, wisdom, and insight, and reveals his will to us, making us his partners in the creation of his will on earth.

The Gift of a Father

After the destruction of Jerusalem and the first Temple in 586 BCE, the author of Lamentations described the people of Israel as "fatherless orphans" (Lamentations 5:3). When pleading with Israel to repent, the prophet Hosea also referred to the nation as "Orphan Israel" (Hosea 14:3b). God's response was a promise to heal them and love them freely (v. 4), and to answer them and care for them (v.8a). Jesus fulfilled that promise.

For the orphans—and we are all orphans eventually, whether by death or because of neglect, abandonment, or lack of love—Jesus provides a loving parent. In fact, Jesus is clear we have one father and one teacher—the Christ (Matthew 23:8-10).

Like a good father, he provides guidance, teaching, structure, and discipline. He offers us a wonderful role model of how to live a life of love, service, and purpose. He gives us protection and a sense of security in his presence. We know, as long as we abide in him, our wolves can't get us. He makes us strong in his strength when we are weak and carries us when we fall.

His arms shelter us during the storms of life. He comforts us in our mourning and gives us an eternal hope to see those we have lost once again. He weeps with us when we weep and rejoices with us when we rejoice. We can hide in him when we need time to recover and heal. He holds us when we need encouragement.

He doesn't turn to us to meet his needs or use us for his purposes—you may need to stop and think about that one for a moment, because some "church" language has made it sound like "it's not about us" at all but is about us fulfilling some purpose. I strongly disagree with that kind of language. He created us for relationship, not to produce outcomes. His only desire is for our good.

Without him, we wouldn't know what genuine love is, for human love carries some expectation of return, while his love is pure and without condition or requirement of reciprocity. Yes, he loves even those of his children who reject him or don't believe him. He pursues all of his children to their last breath—and perhaps even beyond, as it is not his will that any of his children are lost. He loves us completely, exactly as we are. And he loves us enough to not want to leave us exactly as we are but works with us and in us for our growth, spiritual maturity, righteousness, and holiness.

He never puts himself first or makes demands of us. Everything he does, every word he says, and every way he leads us is for our good. Even his discipline is loving, gentle, and filled with grace—never harsh or punitive. I love this verse, which describes beautifully how he parents us: "Take my yoke on you and learn from me, because I am gentle and humble in heart, and you will find rest for your souls" (Matthew 11:29).

The Gift of Spiritual Fruit

Because he is such a wonderful father, we want to be like him. He gives us a mirror in which to see ourselves in truth, and at the same time, he mirrors for us how to best live our lives. His pursuit of us strengthens our deep desire to be close to him. His unbridled, unrelenting love for us fosters in us a deep love for him.

Through our shared experiences, our relationship with him develops deep roots and blossoms with spiritual fruit. His Spirit in us is the source of all spiritual fruit, so the fruit of our lives are gifts from him. These fruits are listed in Galatians 5:22-23.

In addition to finding rest for our souls, we find love. Love and belonging are some of our most basic needs. As I've said repeatedly, God created us for relationship. In the absence of love, we literally wither away. Did you know children who receive no love or nurturance can become what is called "non-organic failure to thrive," meaning their growth and development are delayed due to the emotional deprivation?

Adults also respond strongly to a loss of love. You've probably heard of "broken heart syndrome" where the individual suffers from stress cardiomyopathy due to extreme grief or loss of love. As Proverbs 15:13b states, "by a painful heart the spirit is broken." Suffice it to say, human beings need love, and God gives it in abundance.

In order to give love to others as a spiritual fruit, we must first receive love. Whatever love exists within us to pour out into others' lives originated with God's love for us. In other words, it takes an input of energy to produce more energy. Think of love like fuel. The tank needs to be filled to run the generator. If the generator is going to produce any energy, it needs fuel before it can start. But once the tank is full, the spark ignites, and the engine is able to pour out energy. Our ability to love is dependent on God, as he is the source of all love. His very nature is love.

We also receive the spiritual fruit of joy. The Scriptures are full of references to the absolute, overwhelming joy of being in God's presence, so we know the source of joy. But what is the importance of joy? Do we need joy in the same way that we need love?

Joy was the response of Mary, of Elizabeth's baby in the womb, of the shepherds, and of the angels at Christ's coming. Jesus described the joy in heaven over the repentance of one soul. He proclaimed the joy of the man who discovered treasure hidden in the field and sold all he had to possess the field—meaning the treasure of the Kingdom of God and everything connected to it. The disciples expressed exuberant joy when Jesus came to them after the resurrection. It seems clear joy is directly connected to wonderful things. Does that make it important? Valuable?

After proclaiming his love, he said, "I have told you these things so that my joy may be in you, and your joy may be complete" (John 15:11), so not only is joy associated with wonder, it is directly tied to love. Clearly, Jesus desired his disciples to experience joy—and not only joy, complete joy. Jesus also told his disciples they would rejoice when they saw him again, and no one would be able to take their joy away. From these verses, we can glean that joy is important to Jesus.

Jesus repeatedly instructed his followers to rejoice, and Paul repeated this instruction, including rejoicing even in suffering. But why would joy be important, especially in the midst of suffering?

In the Old Testament we find our answer. Nehemiah 8:10b tells us, "the joy of the Lord is your strength." I Chronicles 16:27b reiterates the connection between strength and joy and reveals the source of both as God. If joy strengthens us, can you see how rejoicing, even during suffering, would be both an important and valuable fruit to us?

Jesus describes how a woman birthing a child suffers great distress, but when the child is born, she forgets her suffering because of her joy in receiving her child (John 16:21). In the same way, joy strengthens us and helps us recover from our suffering. Research into joy has demonstrated that joy and resilience are two sides of the same coin. One feeds and reinforces the other. Joy strengthens us to keep going. As Helen Keller famously observed, "Your joy and you shall form an invincible host against difficulties."

At the heart of it, joy makes life worth living. Joy is associated with gratitude and meaning in our lives. Spiritually, joy is a full-bodied expression of the goodness of God. In addition, joy has physiological benefits, including decreased blood pressure, a healthier immune system, and a longer life.

Joy is fundamentally about relationship and connection. Joy is for sharing. We need love and belonging, and when we perceive we are receiving love in our lives, we feel joy. We also feel joy when those we love experience joy. Joy is contagious and intrinsically reinforcing.

Joy is also connected to hope. When we perceive good things that we have longed or hoped for, we feel joy. Finally, joy is about abundance. When we perceive we are receiving more than we think we deserve or have expected, we feel joy. Do you see the characteristics of God in these descriptions of joy? As Proverbs 10:28a states, "The hope of the righteous is joy."

Another fruit of Christ's presence within us is peace. Like love and joy, peace brings many benefits, both physiological and emotional. Inner peace actually helps our brain to develop, which helps fight against the mental decline associated with aging. It improves digestion, strengthens our immune system, and has many benefits for heart health.

Peace also improves our patience, compassion, and tolerance while decreasing our levels of anger. As a result, peace provides great benefit to our functioning well in relationships. It increases positivity, which helps with overall mental health. Peace helps our ability to focus which helps us work toward our goals. Our vision is clearer when we are at peace. Most importantly, we can hear God better from a place of peace and centeredness.

According to John, Christ's final words to his disciples were about peace. "Peace I leave with you; my peace I give to you" (John 14:27a). He confirms he wasn't speaking of an external peace, as the world might seek, but inner peace brought by his presence through the Holy Spirit. When Jesus appeared to his disciples after his resurrection, he greeted them once again with peace, so it appears peace was significant to Jesus. But what is its significance?

Paul believes peace acts as a kind of guard over our hearts and minds, which is in congruence with the effects of peace mentally and physically. But I believe peace acts as a warning signal, similar to how pain warns us of physical damage. We feel peace in God's presence, but lie beliefs disrupt our peace. If we can develop an expectation of peace, meaning our normal is God's peace beyond understanding, then when our peace is disrupted, we'll notice and ask Jesus what lie belief is causing the disruption.

Now, you might be thinking, a lot of things disrupt my peace, not just my lie beliefs. What about other people's actions? What about circumstances?

Have you considered the reasons why other people's actions and circumstances have the power to disrupt your peace? The power comes from *your interpretation and perception* of the actions and circumstances. For example, if someone acts rudely toward me, I can either internalize their behavior—in other words, I can make their rudeness about me—or I can recognize their rudeness is their choice and has nothing to do with me. My *perception and interpretation* of their action determines my *feelings*.

The same is true of my circumstances. If I interpret hardship as a personal assault, my peace will certainly be disrupted. If I perceive hardship as part of living in a fallen world and focus on choosing my responses based on truth and love, I can remain in peace.

So, peace informs me. It enlightens me. It warns me when my interpretation is faulty, and my perception is inaccurate. When I start to lose my peace, I'm able to go to Jesus for a new interpretation or altered perception, and he will restore my peace. In this way, peace acts as a guard over my heart and mind.

Peace can help me live a transcendent life, where the actions of others and the worldly circumstances lose their power. If I allow his peace to inform me and trust the peace of his presence is always present in me, I'm able to deflect lie beliefs before they take hold.

Patience is another gift from God's Spirit within us. We know patience comes from God because Scripture repeatedly describes God's patience and forbearance with Israel, with the disciples, and with us. In addition, both Old and New Testament verses admonish us to wait patiently on the Lord, so he knows the value and benefits of patient living.

The first Biblical descriptor of love is patience, which means a lack of patience indicates a dearth of love. Impatience often arises from having unmet expectations, resulting in stress, anger, and frustration, whereas patience is more accepting, flexible, and free. The ability to delay gratification improves our decision-making ability, for when we make our choices based on immediacy, we often set ourselves up for long-term disappointment and frustration. Patient people are less depressed and more hopeful overall.

Impatience also arises from a belief in control. Remember, control is an illusion, so when we seek control or believe we have it, we will be frustrated. Relinquishing our belief in control allows God's patience to flow freely from us toward others and toward circumstances in our lives. It enables us to release our need to determine outcomes and accept those things we can't change.

Paul indicates that Jesus said, "It is more blessed to give than to receive" (Acts 20:35b), although those words as spoken by Jesus do not show up in any other place in Scripture. However, Matthew 10:8b is a similar instruction: "Freely you have received; freely give." The directive to give to the poor, the widow, the orphan, and the resident foreigner occurs throughout Scripture. These acts of kindness are reflections, albeit poor ones, or God's wealth of kindness toward us.

According to Paul, God's kindness leads us to repentance. By the same token, a lack of kindness indicates someone has turned away from God, because having received so much kindness, only a hardened heart would refuse to pass it on. Similarly, Jesus instructed us to love our enemies because we see that God is kind to ungrateful, evil people—like us.

Kindness as a spiritual fruit increases self-esteem, empathy, and compassion. It improves the overall mood and boosts confidence and optimism. Like peace, kindness is contagious and intrinsically reinforcing. Acts of kindness improve our emotional well-being.

Often, kindness loses out to the urgent and the immediate. We get busy and don't take the time to include simple acts of kindness as a part of our daily lives. But busyness increases stress while kindness is a stress eliminator. Kindness goes a long way in healing damaged relationships, but when we don't respond in kindness to our enemies as Jesus instructs, we feed the division and anger between us. The world is reaping, both physically and emotionally, what it is sowing.

The fruit of gentleness softens our heart, allowing us to see and accept the other person for who they are. It opens us up to others in a way that deepens and strengthens relationships. It creates a space for both parties in the relationship to flourish, and it promotes forgiveness. So, you can see why God provides gentleness as one of his gifts.

These same qualities of gentleness apply to us. When we are gentle with ourselves, we can more readily see who we truly are. We create space for ourselves to grow, rest, and rejuvenate. We deepen our understanding of ourselves and are more likely to forgive ourselves for our failings. Gentleness helps us slow down so we can hear God. All these things promote healthier relationships and healthier attitudes.

The gentleness of Jesus is best understood in his identification as the good shepherd who carries the lambs in his arms, who feeds and cares for his flock, and who rescues his sheep from the pit, even on the Sabbath. Recall how he described himself as gentle and humble in heart and associated those traits with finding rest for our souls. If we are called to be more and more like Christ, we must resist the pressures and harshness of the world and receive his gentleness in our spirits so that same gentleness will flow out toward others.

Peter described inner beauty as "a gentle and tranquil spirit, which is precious in God's sight" (I Peter 3:4). James informs us that wisdom brings gentleness. Paul exhorts us repeatedly to let our gentleness be evident at all times. We are even told to restore the person discovered in sin with a spirit of gentleness and to carry one another's burdens. Through these many calls to gentleness, we can see how much value Jesus places on this gift.

"Taste and see that the Lord is good" (Psalm 34:8). In this phrase, we are invited to "eat a little" and realize, from the smallest experience, the great goodness of God. As with the other spiritual fruit, he shares his goodness with us.

Paul tells us the fruit of the light exists in all goodness, righteousness, and truth. In other words, we are not "good"—no one is good except God—but the fruit of his goodness grows in us through the presence of his Spirit. In this way, goodness is godliness, reflections of God's presence seen as righteousness and holiness.

True goodness is selfless, like Christ is selfless in all he does. The Greek word for goodness means having an upright heart and life. Spiritual goodness isn't about good behavior—it refers to an internal state of being. And it isn't something we can create by trying hard to be good. None of our efforts can change the fundamental self-centeredness of our hearts because of the sin of Eden.

But Christ in us and the work of his Spirit in our lives can transform our hearts and make them upright. Goodness is evident in a changed character, not just changed behavior. This form of goodness benefits others more than ourselves. God's goodness is merciful and gracious, righteous and just, tender and gracious, strong and enduring. When God's goodness permeates us within, our hearts will experience these qualities, not by our effort but by his presence.

Being good does have benefits for us as well. Our overall emotional well-being improves when we are good. Our motives are changed, and as Christ points out when he expounded on the true meaning of the law—for example, the law says do not commit adultery, but Jesus said if you lust, you've committed adultery *in your heart*—the motive behind an action is more significant than the action itself.

Another benefit is when we treat others well, with respect, mercy, and grace, they are more likely to reciprocate. Of course, this isn't always the case, and if our motive in being good is to get treated better, good fruit will not result. Bad root, bad fruit. If we are led by his Spirit, our heart motive will be to become more like Christ.

The fruit of faithfulness is often misunderstood as just having faith. However, the Greek word here also refers to reliability, meaning we are trustworthy and reliable in our ways, just as God demonstrates faithfulness throughout Scripture. In other words, faith goes both ways. The fruit of *pistis* believes and trusts God and is also believable and trustworthy before God. The spiritual gift of faithfulness mentioned here reflects an attitude of faith in all things.

Jesus described a faithful and wise slave as one whom the master finds doing his job when he returns home. This slave is blessed, and the master will put him in charge of all of his possessions as a result of his faithfulness. But Jesus also describes an evil slave as believing the master will not return for a long time, so he abuses the other slaves and eats, drinks, and carouses. That master will cast out this slave to a place of weeping and gnashing of teeth.

This parable was told in the context of Christ describing the signs of his coming, so you can see how the faithful slave, like the five wise virgins, is prepared. His attitude is hopeful and expectant of the master's return—he has faith in his master—and he is faithful to his assigned task from his master. But this parable is also relevant to the fruit of faithfulness beyond just waiting for Christ's return. Remember, the slave trusted his master and was trustworthy and reliable for his master. If the fruit of faithfulness is in evidence, we, too, will reflect these attitudes. And God will trust us with his Kingdom.

An attitude of faithfulness comes from our connection with the Holy Spirit, for our hearts tend to be more self-serving than other-serving, and a self-serving heart is likely to be tempted to act as the evil slave. If we believe we receive immediate gain from beating the servants and turning to revelry, we'll likely do it. We don't trust the master to be reliable. Only fear of the master's punishment would keep us from doing what serves us in the moment.

But the faithful and wise slave serves out of love for the master and desire to do his job well. He isn't expecting the master's reward, nor is he doing his job in hopes of getting special treatment. He wants to serve, and he serves from a heart of love.

When we are one with Christ, faithful service to God and others flows from us freely. Our hearts, filled with his love, serve because we love, not for personal gain of any kind. We don't expect appreciation or reward because those things don't reflect our motive. We have no expectation of personal gain. Expectations place demands on others. Instead, we desire to be faithful in our pouring out, and God is faithful in pouring into us. Paul describes an attitude of faithfulness well:

> "Instead of being motivated by selfish ambition or vanity, each of you should, in humility, be moved to treat one another as more important than yourself. Each of you should be concerned not only about your own interests, but about the interests of others as well. You should have the same attitude toward one another that Christ Jesus had" (Philippians 2:3-5).

The final fruit of the Spirit listed by Paul is often translated self-control, but this is a poor rendering of the Greek. The Greek word, *egkrateia,* is literally translated dominion from within. It refers to having the ability to restrain fleshly urges and operate in moderation instead of indulgence. Note how these descriptors do not indicate control.

Paul is asking who has dominion within us? Is it our flesh, with its sinful desires? According to Paul, when the flesh has dominion, we can't do good. "For those who live according to the flesh have their outlook shaped by the things of the flesh...for the outlook of the flesh is death" (Romans 8:5a, 6a). The flesh is openly hostile and rebellious toward God.

Or are we surrendered to his Spirit within us? Have we given our will to him? Are we "shaped by things of the Spirit"? If so, the fruit of the Holy Spirit is in evidence in us. Do we belong to Jesus? Are we his children, the children of the promise, grafted in branches who live through the vine? If we are, his Spirit will have dominion within us.

Egkrateia also indicates temperance or balance in life. His presence keeps our perspective balanced and not prone to extremes, according to the way he lived his life here—for example, not taking the law to extremes and thus missing the purpose of the law, but instead living by the heart of the law. In the extremes we evidence rigidity, judgment, black-and-white thinking, harshness, and control.

One of the characteristics of resilient people is they don't operate in extremes. They remain flexible and adaptable. They recognize that adversity doesn't last forever, so they don't tend to overreact and catastrophize. They don't have unrealistic expectations, like believing things will be perfect. They accept that things are going to change and keep a positive attitude even when problems arise.

When we operate in moderation and temperance, under the dominion of the Holy Spirit, we demonstrate flexibility, malleability, and softness. We do not make judgments against others, because we do not judge ourselves harshly. We operate in the realm of choice and responsibility instead of control, knowing when we err, we can always make a different choice, and taking responsibility for our choices instead of blaming others. And we operate in grace, because of God's extravagant grace for us.

Do you see how all of these gifts of the fruit of the Spirit I've discussed so far benefit *us* as much as they benefit others? God's gifts are always for our good, but what is also amazing to me is how God manages to bring good for others out of those things that are good for me. It is certainly true that all good things come from the Father.

The Gifts of Beauty and Creativity

Have you looked outside? Really looked? God has surrounded us with beauty. He's given us every kind of environment imaginable to enjoy, enough to fulfill every individual preference. Such majesty and serenity and magnificence and simplicity, all at the same time, is beyond our ability to describe. He said so himself when he called his creation good.

When God challenged Job, he wove verses of poetry expounding on the wonders of his creation, from the furthest stars to the unseen depths, from the tiniest creature's birth to the birth of the planet. His reply silenced Job's why questions, as he realized he had no ground from which to speak. The extent of God's creativity knows no bounds. He transcends our temporal questions, and like Job, we are left filled with wonder and awe in the face of a creation beyond our comprehension.

The same God who flung the stars in the heavens and restrained the oceans created *us*. He made us in his image, containing within us different aspects of the beauty of his nature, and set us free to explore, develop, imagine, and create. Yes, God chose to make us partners in the act of creation. He gifted us with creativity in a vast plethora of forms and expressions. What an incredible gift from the Creator—to be willing to share the miraculous act of creation with the created.

Imagine what it would be like if we didn't have imagination. Oh, wait…if you didn't have imagination, you couldn't imagine it, could you? But since you do have imagination, picture living life without the ability to make decisions or problem-solve or plan or set goals or predict consequences or dream or see possibilities or hope (yes, hope requires imagination) or create or innovate or understand life and people beyond our own concrete experiences or have empathy—or *faith*?

Imagine living without art or music or books or movies or dance or plays or photography. Then go deeper and notice all the things in your home that would disappear if we had no imagination—from fabrics to technology, everything you see, including your home, was first imagined before it was created.

Now imagine a life without beauty. Imagine holding your newborn child, and the only thing you see is a wrinkled, red-faced creature instead of the most beautiful creation you've ever seen. Imagine looking into the eyes of a loved one and only seeing an orb. Look out your window and delete everything you find beautiful or lovely, anything that adds color and depth and joy and wonder—and see how you feel about what's left.

Through our imagination, we are able to create new and different expressions reflecting the beauty of God's creation, allowing us to share in his creative process and connect with his heart. God chose to give us vision beyond our physical eyes, and without it, our lives would consist of a series of genetically encoded responses geared toward survival. Instinct without evaluation. Action without choice. No chance at growth or betterment of ourselves. No hope.

So, if you think you are lacking in imagination and creativity and beauty, think again. You use your imagination every second of every day in making decisions and choosing based on consequences. You create each time you hope or dream or plan for the future. Your beauty shines in your reflection of God's nature as his child created in his image.

And if you're having a rough day and can't think of items for your gratitude list, remember imagination and creativity and beauty. These amazing gifts are vital to every aspect of our lives.

The Gift of Truth

In our postmodern world, we question if absolute truth exists and rely on "our truth"—our transient, changeable, unreliable truth—to direct our path. For us, truth changes based on context, depending on our interpretation and individual perspective, which leaves us unanchored and twisting in the wind of circumstance.

As a result, our wolves have easy access to us. Nothing grounds us. We have no way to fight them off, no weapons that work to keep them at bay. Without absolute truth, how can we be sure of anything? The truth is—yes, pun intended—we can't.

I believe the postmodern assertion that truth is not absolute is the single most dangerous and destructive belief our enemy has deceived us into embracing.

Jesus says he is the truth. He told Pilate his purpose in coming into the world was to testify to the truth. Pilate's response makes it sound as if he didn't believe in truth. But Jesus had already answered his question, "What is truth?" when he told his disciples he was the truth.

Jesus' life evidences the truth for us. If he lives in us, the truth lives in us. So, if we are one with him and through our connection and relationship with him come to know who he is, we know the truth. If through knowing who he is, we come to know who we are, we know the truth. The truth is certain and sure. It grounds us and anchors us to a solid foundation.

In the *truest* sense of the word, when I say the truth is a gift from God, I am saying Jesus is our gift from God—which takes us all the way back to the opening section on his presence being our greatest gift.

The truth is always true, meaning Jesus is always the same. We can be certain of him. Those characteristics we see evidenced in his life—his continuous presence, his deep love, his ability to see us and know who we are, his humility—will never change. He will always defend us and lead us. His revelation is trustworthy. His redemption will always come. He is *always* the bread of life, the light of the world, the true vine, the living water, and our good shepherd. We can rely on these things.

I've talked about how Jesus is the *logos,* the transcendent eternal, the unchanging universal truth, the divine nature. Nothing exists without him. Whatever *is*, is him. "In him was life" (John 1:4a). He is all, and if he is all, he is absolute. He is eternal, not transient or temporary. His nature is unwavering.

I've also talked about how deception is our enemy's only weapon. Jesus came as our shepherd to take on our wolves and fight for us, to rescue us from their clutches. He came to testify to the truth so that we could live in his truth and be transformed by his truth to become more like him. Do you see why our wolves are so invested in lies?

Jesus said, "you will know the truth, and the truth will set you free" (John 8:32), but what he was essentially saying is, "if you know me, I will set you free." His truth within us equips us for the battle, which is essentially the fight between truth and lie, between good and evil. Through his truth within us, we are able to identify and reject all things that are not of God's Kingdom and keep our minds on whatever is pure and just and lovely and excellent and praiseworthy.

When the winds of circumstance try to blow us over, the truth gives us stability and the strength to stand. If peace is the guard over our hearts and minds, truth is the shield that blocks our wolves from having access to our hearts and minds. As we grow in oneness with Christ and become more like him, the truth permeates our being, replacing the lies we believe and cleansing us of the shroud that covers our identity. Through his presence within us, we can know him, and by knowing him, we can know our true selves. In all these ways, his truth sets us free.

The Gift of Freedom

I often contemplate what the world would be like if God had chosen a different design for his creation of the tapestry of life. I think we tend to take for granted the intricacies of his weaving. Each strand connects to the others to form a complex, masterful pattern that falls apart if one key element fails.

All of the shepherd's gifts are crucial to our lives, but the key element holding everything together is his gift of freedom.

Freedom wasn't mandatory for creation to exist. God could've designed a world without freedom—if he created it contrary to his own nature. We could all be little robots on autopilot, bowing at God's feet without understanding who he is or why he deserves our worship and praise. I suppose we could survive without love or faith or hope or trust—or anything else that requires of us a choice.

But would we want to?

Had God chosen a tapestry woven with the thread of control, this world would look quite different. First, personal authority would not exist, so I would have no ability to choose, no individual personality, and no form of self-expression. Basically, I would lose any form of individual identity. Nothing about me would be unique. What would be worth loving, then?

But that's not the worst of it. Without personal authority, love would not even exist. Love must be chosen. For love to exist, freedom must be its foundation. Love's nature means it must be freely given and freely received, or it becomes something else entirely.

If we have no authority, no individuality, and no love, we can't have faith. Faith requires the ability to choose to trust and believe and love. Without freedom, we have no choice in any of those elements of faith, so we have no faith. And without faith, we have no hope.

Now, we reach the twist in the tapestry. God created us to be free, but we used our freedom to choose to bind ourselves as slaves to sin. We still had free *will*, but we lived our lives in bondage by that will, for we willed to sin. As Jesus explained, "I tell you the solemn truth, everyone who practices sin is a slave of sin. (John 8:34). So, despite our God-ordained freedom, we still lived as slaves.

But God is our redeemer. He provided a way for his tapestry to be restored. The hole created in it by our chosen loss of freedom can be filled, if we choose for it to be. Jesus came and set us free from our slavery to sin, and the freedom he offers us is true and complete freedom. "The slave does not remain in the family forever, but the son remains forever. So if the son sets you free, you will be really free" (v. 35-36).

We tore God's tapestry. Because of our choice, our wolves usurped our personal authority. They covered over our individual identity with lies and urged us to hide our true nature behind walls to "protect" ourselves. Love for us became a relational economy, with expectations attached and payment due. Our faith became porous, weak, and small, so much so Jesus lamented, "when the Son of Man comes, will he find faith on earth?" (Luke 18:8b). And our hope was lost.

God wasn't satisfied with leaving this tapestry torn. I suppose he could've allowed us to live and die in bondage—but like a tapestry woven with the thread of control instead of freedom, allowing his children to continue in slavery would've been contrary to his nature. Instead, God in his freedom made a choice to restore our opportunity to experience freedom and all that comes with it.

Like Adam and Eve, who had a choice and chose slavery, we once again have the gift of freedom to choose. But God will not choose for us, because his tapestry is woven with the thread of freedom, and as we've seen, if freedom is lost, the tapestry falls apart.

In our freedom, will we choose slavery, or will we choose to remain free? Will we choose to live in oneness with Christ, intertwining our lives inextricably with his? Will we allow Jesus to cut the threads of sin away which leave holes in the tapestry of our lives?

The choice is ours.

Questions
1. What gifts of the shepherd do you recognize in your life?

2. In what ways do you experience the four things his presence provides?
3. What spiritual fruit do you see evidenced in your life? What spiritual fruit do you seem to be missing or struggling to evidence?
4. What impact does beauty, creativity, and imagination have in your daily life? In what ways do you express each of these gifts?
5. Jesus has woven truth and freedom into the tapestry of your life. What sins are eating away at your freedom? What truth do you need from Jesus to set you free?

Prayer

Precious Lord Jesus, thank you for your many gifts. Thank you for your provision, your righteousness which transforms me and makes me holy, your many promises, and the indwelling of your Spirit so I can know you and know who I am.

Lord, I have felt like an orphan for so long. Welcome me as your child and embrace me, shelter me, comfort me, and lead me in your ways. Thank you for being my Father. Fill me with your Spirit because I want the fruit of your presence to flow freely from me into the world. Show me my beauty as your creation. Enliven my imagination as I embark on being a co-creator with you. Help me to see and express your creativity within me. Lord, cut the strands of sin that strive to keep me in bondage as a slave. Help me to embrace your truth so I may know freedom in its fullness. In your beautiful name, Amen.

Donna E. Lane, Ph.D.

FOLLOWING THE SHEPHERD

"If anyone wants to become my follower, he must deny himself, take up his cross, and follow me. For whoever wants to save his life will lose it, but whoever loses his life because of me will find it" (Matthew 16:24-25).

What does it mean to be a follower?

To follow means to go or come after, to move behind someone or something and go where he, she, or it goes, to pursue, and to move in the same direction. The definition of a follower is one in service to another, who follows the opinions and teaching of another, and imitates another.

Early in his ministry, when Jesus called on Peter and the other disciples to follow, he was asking them to come with him and go where he was going. Later, Jesus made a distinction between following and being a follower. To become a follower meant certain things needed to change in the individual.

It meant becoming something else—such as a fisher of people instead of fish. It meant a new set of priorities and a new way of doing things—like letting the dead bury their own dead and putting your hand to the plow without looking back. It meant accepting difficult truths and trusting when you didn't understand—for example, when Jesus told them the one who eats his flesh and drinks his blood will live.

It meant getting to know the shepherd because sheep won't follow the voice of a stranger.

The word used by Jesus when he called Peter and the disciples was *akoloutheó*, which means to accompany. But when speaking of becoming followers, Jesus used a different phrase, a phrase used in both the literal and metaphorical sense to mean to come after, having more of a connotation of pursuit and imitation. So, you can also see in the Greek the difference between following and being a follower.

Jesus' instructions on what it takes to become a follower comes on the heels of Peter's strong rebuke when Jesus shared what was to occur in Jerusalem at the hands of the chief priest and elders. Peter said, "This must not happen to you!" to which Christ replied, "Get behind me, Satan! You are a stumbling block to me, because you are not setting your mind on God's interests, but on man's" (Matthew 16:22b-23). The key question here is what was Peter focused on, his self-interest or God's? According to Jesus, Peter's reaction was self-centered, which moves us directly into the reason for Jesus' instruction.

If we examine Jesus' description of what must occur to become a follower of Christ, we find three distinct considerations. His first instruction to the disciples was to deny themselves. Now, Jesus was not talking about living a life of deprivation where any form of self-expression or pursuit of your heart's desires is forbidden. Quite the contrary. Jesus desires an abundant life for us, including the full expression of our true, God-given identity, free from the bondage of sin. Here, Jesus is speaking of denial of the self as God in our lives—the origin of all sin.

We must deny the idea that we can be like God. We must admit we cannot save ourselves, and that our righteousness does not come by our own efforts or abilities. We must surrender our illusion of control and operate in dependence on Christ. We must let go of our self-protection, self-reliance, and self-determination. We must confess our sheep-ish lack of knowledge and turn instead to Jesus for wisdom.

The second instruction is to take up their cross. We must keep in mind as we consider what Jesus means that his taking up the cross had not yet occurred, and he had not shared with the disciples the means of his death, only the fact of its coming. So, what was Jesus trying to convey?

This instruction involves a death—not necessarily a physical death, although almost all the disciples were ultimately killed for their beliefs. It involves the death of clinging to their lives, for Jesus completes this instruction with this explanation: "For whoever *wants to* save his life will lose it"—meaning when we cling to our lives it slips through our fingers—"but whoever loses his life because of me will find it"—in other words, when we willingly release our lives to Jesus, we find true life.

Jesus is asking which we desire more—to save our lives or to have his life in us?

Jesus also refers to their willingness to die for what they believe, because he knew his followers would be threatened with death by their persecutors, as he warned them. But primarily he describes an internal process of release. The more I want to be in control of my own life, the more I lose. The more I let go, the more life I find.

Allowing Jesus to be our shepherd and lead us in all ways doesn't guarantee us an easy life, but it does guarantee us a spiritually fulfilled and eternal life. Releasing our lives to Christ promises a form of death—the death of our flesh or sin nature. But clinging to our lives guarantees a different kind of death—the death of our spirit.

Paul describes himself as crucified to the world, and the world as crucified to him (Galatians 6:14b). He follows up by saying, "the only thing that matters is a new creation!" (v. 15b). He shows us an example of losing his life because of Jesus—the old has died, the new is come.

The third instruction is to follow Jesus. We are to walk where he walks, see as he sees, and be as he is. We are to be imitators of Christ, just as Paul said he was, and keep his teachings. We are to pursue relationship fervently, passionately, and without restraint.

So, what evidence will we see if we become true followers?

Characteristics of a Follower

In Ephesians 3:16-18, Paul describes the inner state of being necessary to become a follower of Christ:

> "I pray that according to the wealth of his glory he will grant you to be strengthened with power through his Spirit in the inner person, that Christ will dwell in your hearts through faith, so that, because you have been rooted and grounded in love, you will be able to comprehend with all the saints what is the breadth and length and height and depth, and thus to know the love of Christ that surpasses knowledge, so that you will be filled up to all the fullness of God."

First, a follower must recognize they can't operate in their own strength. Only by the power of the Holy Spirit can we become true followers of Christ. The presence of his power is experienced in the inner person, not externally, so we aren't to look for miraculous events or external answers to prayer as evidence of the Holy Spirit in our inner being. Those signs and wonders may come, but they are evidence of the Holy Spirit's presence so *others* will believe, not so we will believe.

Second, Christ must dwell in the heart of a follower. We can't become a follower of Christ based on our knowledge of Scripture or from following the teaching of a pastor. Knowing about Jesus isn't enough. We must invite him into our hearts through faith, to live in union with us and, through relationship, become one with him.

Third, love must be our anchor. Our breath and our nature must flow from his heart of love. We must know his love, and from being filled with his love, love will flow from us—love for God first, which then equips us to love ourselves and our neighbors. And more than just knowing his love, we must know the full extent of his love for us, so we may be filled completely with his presence. The breadth and length and height and depth of Christ's love can only be known through intentional, personal experiences with him.

Paul follows up his description of the inner person of a follower with a discussion on the walk of a follower:

> "I...urge you to live worthily of the calling with which you have been called, with all humility and gentleness, with patience, putting up with one another in love, making every effort to keep the unity of the Spirit in the bond of peace...to lay aside the old man who is being corrupted in accordance with deceitful desires, to be renewed in the spirit of your mind, and to put on the new man who has been created in God's image—in righteousness and holiness that comes from truth...(and) be kind to one another, compassionate, forgiving one another, just as God in Christ also forgave you" (Ephesians 4:1-3, 22b-24, 32).

I have selected key elements to focus on in this section of Scripture to capture Paul's overarching message, but I encourage you to read the entirety of Ephesians 4. He has a lot of important, beneficial instruction on what it means to live in unity and holiness.

Paul's first characteristic of a worthy follower is humility, which isn't surprising. Do you recall our discussion on Christ's character found in Philippians 2:5-11, in which Paul expresses the humility and servant nature of Christ? It stands to reason, then, that becoming a follower would mean having the character of Christ, which includes being humble and not considering ourselves equal with God—emptying ourselves as Christ did and becoming obedient to the point of death.

The second characteristic is gentleness. The Greek word, *epieikes*, used here means "justice beyond ordinary justice." Paul is referring to operating in the spirit of the law, not applying strict or harsh standards to others, but expressing the fruits of the spirit of gentleness and moderation or temperance.

He is urging us to treat others as we would want to be treated, with soft words and gentle direction. We are not to desire retribution for wrongs. Instead, we are to seek reconciliation where possible, and if not possible, to seek peace.

The next characteristic involves another spiritual fruit, the fruit of patience. I view patience as the ability to see beyond the behavior of others to identify two things—first, their true nature, who God created them to be, and second, the deeper lies which are the actual reasons for their actions. If I can seek these things with Christ's help, I will feel empathy and compassion for them, which in turn fuels the fruit of patience in me.

Another word for patience is long-suffering, meaning I am willing to "suffer" or tolerate their misbehavior. This is the element Paul describes as "putting up with one another in love." In no way does he mean affirming or reinforcing their misbehavior—Christ would never suggest such a thing. But like Christ, we are to be patient with it, understanding the root causes, and if they are willing, coming alongside them to support them as they address the root causes with Jesus.

It helps tremendously to see both the lies in operation and the true nature of the individual with whom you are struggling. First, it lets you know their misbehavior is not about you, but about their lies. It also helps your patience by helping you love them, as you see them through Christ's eyes and love them as he does, based on who they are, not what they do.

Paul then urges us to maintain the unity of the Spirit in the bond of peace. As he explains, there is one body and one Spirit, one hope, one Lord, one faith, one baptism, and one God. We share this oneness with all believers, in much the same way we share in oneness with Christ.

When division comes, we can know it is from the enemy. Wolves like to cull weaker members of the herd away and divide the herd, making it easier to kill and destroy its members. Our wolves operate in the same manner, using the same tactics. They try to divide and conquer, hoping to leave some members of our community of believers unprotected and unsupported in the wild. When that happens, we become easy prey.

Jesus equips us for unity with a variety of spiritual gifts which are present to build up the body of Christ and bring all to maturity and depth of relationship with Jesus. To maintain unity, Paul encourages us to practice the truth in love, and in so doing, grow and build each other up in love. Unity in the Spirit also comes from the bond of peace. In other words, when we maintain peace in ourselves and with others, as we've discussed, peace acts as a guard, a warning sign of a wolf attack. When we stand in unity, like sheep in a herd, we fare much better against our wolves.

Next, we are to lay aside the old. This direction refers back to Christ's instruction to lay down our lives for him, and in so doing, gain our lives. The old must die. Self must be denied. As Jesus said, you can't put new wine into old wineskins, or the old skins will burst and spill out the wine. You can't live with your feet in both kingdoms—God's Kingdom and the realm of this world.

As Mister Miyagi said, "Walk on road, walk left side, safe. Walk right side, safe. Walk middle, sooner or later, squish like grape." (I'm certainly dating myself here. And if you don't know who Mister Miyagi is, you need to watch the first Karate Kid movie from 1984…would Yoda have been a better choice?)

As the old self dies, we are renewed in our spirit and mind. The new self is revealed—the person created in God's image, our true identity in Christ. However, calling it new is somewhat of a misnomer. It is new in the sense that it has been covered up and hidden by the flesh and the shroud of lies. It is new in that it is different from the old expression of ourselves, which was tainted by the presence of pride and a desire to be our own God.

But our true selves existed from our creation. Before we were born, Christ knew us, intimately and completely. Nothing was hidden from him. So, while the new self is new to us, it isn't new to Christ. It is our first resurrection—the rebirth of our spirit, just as Christ described when he said we must be born again. Out of the death of self comes new life, and this new life lives in the righteousness and holiness that comes from truth.

Paul calls us to another spiritual fruit, the fruit of kindness to one another. The Greek word used here, *chrestos,* indicates gracious kindness, like the kindness of God toward us. Paul pairs kindness with compassion, which is concern for the pain, suffering, and difficulty of others. As we meet others in their pain with understanding, concern, and kindness, we demonstrate the gracious heart of Christ, who meets us in our suffering, shares our tears, holds our hearts, and walks the path with us.

The final characteristic Paul mentions is forgiveness, with special emphasis on God's forgiveness toward us as seen in Christ for our model of how true forgiveness looks. Jesus emphasized the importance of forgiveness, making it a part of the prayer he taught his disciples to pray. He went on to say, if we forgive, we will be forgiven, but if we do not forgive others, the Father will not forgive our sins.

But why is our forgiveness so important? Isn't Christ's forgiveness sufficient?

The parable of the unforgiving slave demonstrates the problem with unforgiveness. The slave owed his king a massive debt. The king was going to sell the slave, his family, and his possessions to recover a portion of the debt, but the slave begged him for mercy. The story says the king showed compassion, released the slave, and forgave his debt.

The slave turns around and grabs someone who owes him a small debt, chokes him, and demands repayment. When the debtor asks for mercy, the slave refuses and has the man thrown in prison.

What the slave received freely from a heart of grace he refuses to offer to another. While the slave walks free, the man in his debt in bound.

But the story isn't finished. When the king hears about the slave's actions, he is righteously angry. He tells the slave the right way to act, then turns him over to be tortured until he can repay the massive debt he originally owed.

Tortured?! Jesus ends the parable by proclaiming this is what our Father will do if we don't forgive as we have been forgiven—he'll turn us over to be tortured. That doesn't sound like our loving Jesus, does it?

But what is our torture? You recall I said the slave was set free and the debtor left in bondage. Now, Jesus shows us the truth. The slave's failure to forgive his fellow man left *him* in bondage, tortured by carrying the sin of the other person through their lack of forgiveness. Jesus is saying he *turns us over* to the consequences of our own choices—the torture of carrying the weight of another person's sin against us.

The lesson for us here is not about punishment from the king. It is about how our own choices to sin by refusing to offer the mercy extended to us from the king leaves us carrying the other person's "debt" as well as our own. We put ourselves in prison to be tortured by the weight of two people's sins.

This consequence applies in our lives as well. We have been forgiven much. If we don't forgive the sin of others against us, we are choosing to carry the weight of their sin, along with our own. Instead, Jesus tells us to forgive as often as is needed—not dependent on the type or degree of sin, or the number of sins committed against us, but based solely on Christ's great mercy toward us.

These are the characteristics of a follower of Christ: humility, gentleness, patience, long-suffering, love, unity, peace, denial of self, rebirth, kindness, and forgiveness. All of these characteristics flow into us from the Holy Spirit who dwells within us. Without his presence, we can't live out these traits. IF we do not know Christ, we are not rooted and grounded in love. Without being anchored in love, we can't know the expansive love of Christ in full measure. And without being filled to the fullness of God, we can't live worthy of our calling as true followers of Christ.

Wisdom

Jesus consistently contrasts his Kingdom with the realm of this world, giving a number of different examples to make it clear he has nothing in common with the realm of evil. Light vs. darkness. Truth vs. lie. Freedom vs. slavery. Love vs. fear. Good vs. evil. These are a few of the ways he demonstrates the stark difference between the two kingdoms.

As followers of Christ, our path is clearly delineated. We don't have to wrestle with confusion over what is righteous and what is sinful. The two paths do not intersect or cross. There isn't a fork in the road for us to ponder or a divergence from God's path that is pleasing to God. Our struggle is not over *what* God desires for us. He has made it clear. Our inner turmoil is over *if* we are willing to walk his path.

As our hearts contend with our lie beliefs and our spirits grapple with our flesh, we need wisdom to sort out the inner turmoil. God provides his wisdom—to those who ask for it. But more often than not, we try to apply human wisdom to the *if* question and wind up confused, lost, and defeated. Our lies *feel* true to us. The desires of our flesh *feel* imperative to us. For these reasons, Jeremiah 17:9 (NIV) warns us, "the heart is deceitful above all things and beyond cure. Who can understand it?"

The answer to Jeremiah's question is found in the following verse (v. 10a): "I the Lord search the heart and examine the mind." Only Jesus can sort out the messy jumble of our thoughts and feelings and bring enlightenment and discernment where there is only darkness and confusion.

Unfortunately, our primary lie from Eden tells us we know best, so we listen to our feelings and ignore the shepherd's voice. And God, ever respectful, allows us to choose. As Proverbs 1:7 tells us, "Fearing the Lord is the beginning of discernment, but fools have despised wisdom and moral instruction."

Scripture pits human wisdom against the wisdom of God and reveals the foolishness of human wisdom and the depth of the riches of God's wisdom. For example, Paul states, "Has God not made the wisdom of the world foolish? For the foolishness of God is wiser than human wisdom, and the weakness of God is stronger than human strength" (I Corinthians 1:20b, 25).

Paul goes on to say he doesn't speak with the wisdom of this age—meaning the wisdom spoken by Greek philosophers and Hebrew theologians—and he doesn't speak words taught by human wisdom, but he speaks with the wisdom of God and words taught by the Spirit. His conclusion? "For the wisdom of this age is foolishness to God" (I Corinthians 3:19).

The wisdom of God has been personified as a woman in Scripture, namely in Proverbs, Ecclesiastes, Job, and Jesus personified wisdom in Matthew 11:19, Luke 7:35, and Luke 11:49. Wisdom's opposite, folly, enters as a character in these books as well, offering a point-counterpoint similar to the contrast between God's Kingdom and the evil or worldly realm.

A consistent question, from Solomon to Job to Paul, is "where can wisdom be found?" The consistent answer is wisdom is only found in God. According to Paul, Christ became for us wisdom from God (I Corinthians 1:30b).

Wisdom shows up in Proverbs offering blessings, insight, understanding, long life, and prosperity to those who follow her guidance. To possess wisdom is considered most precious. She is regularly associated with the fear of the Lord, meaning to stand in awe, reverence, respect, and adoration of him. In fact, the beginning of wisdom is the fear of the Lord (Proverbs 9:10).

By wisdom, God laid the earth's foundations. It makes sense, then, that wisdom would be a good companion for our journey. She calls out to us and encourages us to eat at her table and walk in the way of understanding. She says the wise listen to her instruction and become wiser still, and a righteous person listens to her teaching and adds to their knowledge. Contrast this with folly, who also calls out to us, telling us it is sweeter to get away with something evil than to enjoy something good, and doing corrupt things in secret is pleasant, but what she doesn't tell us is the dead are the guests in her house.

We need God's help to recognize the difference between wisdom and folly. Thankfully, Christ lives in us, and he is the wisdom of God. Our oneness with Christ offers us complete access to God's wisdom—again, for those who ask for it and seek it.

The confusion and despair reflected in Ecclesiastes and the pain and indignation of Job show us how difficult it can be to recognize wisdom when we are in the throes of suffering or internal torment. Our feelings and doubts muddy the waters. The shroud of lies covers our eyes, making it more difficult to discern. The pain of our suffering screams louder than the call of wisdom. In those times, we tend to wander, lost and blind, leaning on our own understanding.

Job pursues God and doesn't sin, even in his questioning of God and frustration with wisdom's elusiveness, and he receives his answer, although it wasn't the answer he expected. The Teacher in Ecclesiastes wasn't so blessed. Thinking he was using wisdom to discern the purpose and meaning of life, he finds himself in the arms of folly because he trusted in his human wisdom. Like Job, he asks where wisdom can be found, and finally arrives at the same conclusion as the others—wisdom is found in the Creator.

Paul identifies wisdom as one of the spiritual gifts given by God—in fact, lavished on us by the riches of his grace. He also makes it clear as he prays for the church in Ephesus to receive spiritual wisdom and revelation that wisdom comes from a growing knowledge of Christ—meaning the deeper and more connected our relationship is, the more wisdom and revelation we receive. And through God's wisdom, we receive insight into God's will and maturity in our faith.

According to James 3:16-18, we also receive gentleness from wisdom. If you recall the discussion on the meaning of gentleness in the Greek, James is referring to "justice beyond justice", having compassion and empathy rather than harshness and rigidity. He also says God's wisdom is pure, peaceful, accommodating, full of mercy and good fruit, impartial, and not hypocritical, and produces righteousness and peace in us.

But from human wisdom, a wisdom Paul claims has no real value, we learn gratification of the flesh and self-indulgence. James says earthly, natural, or demonic "wisdom" results in bitter jealousy and selfishness, for human wisdom is self-centered by definition since it comes from the self and is therefore tainted by the sin nature and our lie beliefs. This is not true wisdom, but it can seem like wisdom to us as we please ourselves in the moment with no thought to the long-term consequences.

I would suggest that human wisdom has certain identifiable characteristics. I believe human or demonic "wisdom" externalizes—which means blames others for its problems and flaws, refuses responsibility for its actions, and demands others take responsibility for its feelings. Another characteristic I've observed in human or demonic "wisdom" is having expectations of entitlement, looking to others to feed their demands, and feeling owed something by the world.

While God's wisdom is pure and peaceful, human wisdom is selfish and demanding. Where God's wisdom is full of mercy and gentleness, human wisdom blames others. God's wisdom produces righteousness and peace, but human wisdom produces entitlement and bitterness. If we recognize the characteristics and correctly identify when we are using human or demonic "wisdom", we can step off that merry-go-round, ask Jesus to fill our minds and hearts with his wisdom, and change our course. The result will be good fruit in our lives.

Cleaning House

Christ's dwelling place is within us. If we base our understanding of how he views his home by how particular God was about the Temple, I think we can safely say Jesus prefers a clean "house." As a follower of Christ, one of our tasks together will be cleaning our spiritual house—cleaning out the closets, cabinets, and draws, scrubbing the floors, clearing junk out of our basement, washing windows, and making sure everything is spick-and-span.

Studies have found that clutter increases anxiety and a sense of unease in the physical world. I believe the same thing happens in our spirit when our spiritual house is not in order. God isn't characterized by disorder but by peace. If his home is to reflect his character, it'll need some sprucing up.

Over time, we collect a lot of stuff in our spiritual home—much of it undesirable and all of it unnecessary. Beliefs litter our rooms like dust coating the surfaces and dimming our shine. Unresolved conflicts crowd our storage areas. Unforgiven sins against us rot in our refrigerator growing mold., their odor wafting throughout the house and reminding us of our bitterness. Painful memories pile up in our basement. Idols adorn our mantle, our tables, and our walls. Nasty lies hide in the walls and slink around in the corners, waiting for opportunities to jump out and bite us.

Jesus wants to adorn us in white robes and start our Kingdom lives—but there's work to do to ready ourselves. Revelation 7:14 says our robes must be washed in the blood of the Lamb. Washing our robes is a work of Christ and can't be accomplished by our efforts. Those whose robes are washed are blessed and have the right to the tree of life—the symbolic tree opposing the tree of knowledge of good and evil in the garden where Eve took Satan's bait—and may enter the Kingdom by the gates.

This type of apocalyptic language and symbolism can be confusing, so let's take a minute and unpack its meaning. Think about how you clean. You don't use a dirty rag to clean your counters. What would be the point of that? You'll just smear the dirt around, adding more filth to what's already there. No, if you want to clean something, you start with a clean cloth and some form of cleaning solution.

According to I John 1:7 which states, "But if we walk in the light as he himself is the light, we have fellowship with one another and the blood of Jesus his Son cleanses us from all sin", Jesus' blood is our cleaning solution, and his light is our white cloth. His blood is pure—untainted, without sin. His light touches every nook and cranny within us. Nothing is hidden from him. When we receive him in our hearts, his light floods us, and his blood purifies us, leaving us clothed in white, untouched by the stain of sin.

Once we are purified, we need to get rid of all the extraneous junk we collected during our worldly years. Truth is a powerful weightlifter. It can carry those painful memories out into the light, deal with them, and decide if they need to be stored or thrown out. Those dusty beliefs we collected from childhood forward are readily swept away by God's truth when we seek his Spirit in prayer and listen to his voice. Truth is like insecticide to those creepy-crawling lies. It casts those whispering uglies out into the darkness.

Forgiveness is another great mover. It'll put on its white gloves and face the stench to address each container in your fridge, carrying the bag of trash to the curb when it's finished. Forgiveness can also be a big help to Truth as you go through those basement memories.

Idols? Well, Jesus and you will have to deal with those yourselves. They require repentance, receiving forgiveness, and surrender to get rid of them. And man, it can be hard to let them go. Some of them hold a special or meaningful place in your heart—at least you think so. Some of them serve a good purpose—at least in your mind.

So, once again, Jesus will likely call on Truth to step in and help him remind you that the idols in your life foment destruction. Remember the discussion on wisdom and folly? They'll show you why what you believe about needing those idols or wanting those idols isn't true. Then, Jesus will bring in the big guns—Surrender. And Surrender will cart them off once and for all.

The key here is your willingness. Notice I didn't say your discipline or your strength or your efforts. For Jesus to finish the good work of cleaning your house, you must be willing to let go of your old junk and your old ways. Your part of the job is willingness. If you willingly invite Jesus into your home and ask him to help you clean it with his friends, Truth, Forgiveness, and Surrender, he will finish the job.

I refer back to the verses where Jesus taught about the old way and the new way.

> "No one sews a patch of unshrunk cloth on an old garment, because the patch will pull away from the garment and the tear will be worse. And no one pours new wine into old wineskins; otherwise, the skins burst and the wine is spilled out and the skins are destroyed. Instead they put new wine into new wineskins and both are preserved" (Matthew 9:16-17).

These parables were told in the context of the John's disciples questioning the fasting practices of Jesus' disciples, who didn't fast. Jesus' reply used the analogy of wedding guests mourning while the bridegroom was still with them. Jesus is the bridegroom, and his disciples are the wedding guests in his story. Then, he said a time would come when the bridegroom would be taken away and the guests would fast at that time.

This is where Jesus shared the parables of the unshrunk cloth and the new wine. He is saying he is doing something new. His ways—how he is present with us, his teachings, his Kingdom—are not going to be like the old ways. John's disciples and the Pharisees fasted because it was the law. Jesus came to fulfill the law himself, not through fasting or ritual sacrifice but through his sacrifice. His way is a new way. You can't stitch the new way onto the old ways and think it will work. It won't.

In other words, you can't assimilate Jesus—which means taking in new information and making it fit in your existing knowledge. You must accommodate for him—which means altering your existing knowledge to fit the new experience or new information.

When Jesus is taken from the disciples, they will fast, but not because of the law. They will fast because they *mourn*. His new way is about relationship and love, not about the law.

Some theologians suggest the tree of knowledge symbolizes the law, while the tree of life represents relationship with God. One is death, and the other is life. As the Genesis story indicates, you can't eat the fruit from both trees.

In the same way, you can't keep your old ways scattered all over your house, taking up space and distracting you from your relationship with Jesus. If you're going to take in the new way, something has to give.

Hopefully, what gives will be your vise grip on control and your desire to be master over your life. What needs to be crucified is your flesh. What needs to happen is surrendering into dependence.

Surrendering into Dependence

If you recall, I defined surrendering into dependence in Chapter One as:
1. yielding your authority to God's authority;
2. relinquishing your self-sufficiency and self-determination in exchange for his presence, guidance, and love; and
3. trusting your life fully into his hands.

It is complete and total release. It's putting all your chips on his number—all your eggs in his basket. It's going "all in" on God, with nothing held back in reserve—nothing left in your hands.

Exodus 20:5 describes God as jealous, but the word in Hebrew connotes zeal, so a better translation would be our God is a zealous God. The word indicates a passion and intensity for something, a deep, abiding desire to protect and defend. God's command against bowing down to or serving idols isn't because his feelings are hurt, or he feels betrayed. He gives these commands, as with all others, for *our sakes*. He knows if we worship idols, we become slaves to our idols, which leads to our destruction, and his zeal to protect us won't allow that to happen.

In the same way, surrendering into dependence isn't for God's sake. He doesn't need us. He isn't using us. He *wants* us in relationship with him. And he wants that relationship because he loves us and knows how much it benefits us to be in a place of surrender.

At its core, surrendering into dependence is the antidote for the tree of knowledge. It is the death of trying to be gods over our lives.

Are you exhausted from trying to figure things out? Are you sick and tired of feeling like you're always messing up, no matter how hard you try? Are you weighed down under a heavy burden, feeling responsible for everything and everyone? Do you want to surrender? Let's talk about how to let go of the old.

First, we need to acknowledge we can't do anything on our own, including surrendering into dependence. We need Christ's help. In fact, we need him to carry the bulk of the load. Remember, he said, "My yoke is easy to bear, and my burden is not hard to carry" (Matthew 11:30). So, we can know if something feels impossibly hard, we're taking too much on ourselves—more than he intends us to carry.

Our first "new" to adopt is building up the strength of our communication with Jesus. I've mentioned before prayer is a two-way communication., with the primary mode of prayer as listening. We need an altered mindset about the nature of prayer. Think of it more like talking with a friend or your spouse. You want to keep the lines of communication open at all times, not only during set times of day.

In addition, you want to get used to sharing everything. No, you aren't wasting God's time. Remember, he is infinite and eternal. He isn't bound by time or space, so what he offers you is his undivided attention, and he wants to share everything with you. There is no such thing as a detail too insignificant for God. If he knows the count of the hairs on your head, surely he wants to know those things that are meaningful to your life, no matter how small.

I choose to talk with Jesus about everything. I start my day with a "good morning, Jesus" and "what do we have in store for today?" A key here is I take the time to listen to his response and to center myself on him for the rest of the day. The rest of the day proceeds with the same kinds of open communication. While I'm preparing breakfast, I might ask him if he has anything he needs me to know right now. As I'm getting ready for work, I talk with him about my clients and listen for his insights and leading. And on it goes throughout the day.

When I first started this practice of ongoing conversation, I needed reminders because I wasn't used to thinking this way, and I needed his help with the listening process because I was impatient and easily distracted. The so-called imperatives of the world crowded out my focus and time. I struggled with paying attention for his voice and getting my tasks done.

I remember at one point, I was driving down the road, white-knuckle gripping the steering wheel, Christian music blaring from my speakers, repeating the prayer, "Don't let me lose this. Don't let me lose this." I was still believing most of the weightlifting was up to me, and I knew my failings. I was so afraid I would lose my "grip" on Jesus, I was panicky.

What I didn't know is *he* would never let go of *me*.

I found the more I practiced, the more natural ongoing conversation felt. The verse about his sheep knowing his voice became my reality. I learned more about who and how he was through our ongoing conversations, so I gained clarity on what to expect from him. At the same time, the enemy's tactics became more obvious and distinctive from Jesus' ways.

Before long, asking Jesus about everything was my automatic response. I didn't need those little reminders anymore. My focus shifted to becoming more like him, so I began exploring what he needed to change in me to transform me into his likeness. He began to lovingly break my agreements with the enemy, places where I had unwittingly made a pact to believe Satan's deceptions. Jesus shined light on those places in my heart I was holding out as my own and revealed the beliefs that had me ensnared. Then he brought truth to those deep places in my heart and washed away the ugliness of those lies.

Layer after layer he exposed and replaced with truth. And the more he removed, the more I realized my deep, acute need for him.

When he reached the root lie of my trust in my own knowledge, I recognized the true extent of my lack and the tremendous pain in my life caused by that lie. He broke through the morass of entangled vines with his great love. For the first time in my life, I knew I was loved, I mattered, and I had value.

Trust and love filled my heart. I opened my hands and willingly released my heart and my spirit and my mind into his hands.

Next came the process of forgiveness. Now, it is my experience that forgiveness is possible when you still believe lies, but much more difficult. What I found is, when Jesus dealt with my lies, I saw the individuals I needed to forgive through different lenses. Forgiveness was much easier from a place of truth because the sins committed against me no longer had any power. The lies they planted were the only power they had left. Once the lies were gone, their power evaporated, and I was able to release the sin against me into Jesus' hands.

Forgiving myself for all of my mistakes and for believing Satan's lies was another part of the forgiveness process. Christ's grace and mercy were key to letting myself off the hook. After all, if he forgave me and didn't condemn me, who was I to judge myself? I'm not God, so I don't get to be the judge. Do you see how that would've been more difficult if he hadn't broken my grip on my own knowledge?

The lived-out connection through communication and relationship continued, establishing peace where there once was an internal war and wholeness where there once was division. And the deeper this relationship grew, the more I was immersed in his Spirit and the more I became one with him—all through the power of his Spirit. All I did was agree for him to accomplish it.

Surrendering into dependence manifests in us with the presence of his peace, the serenity in your spirit of knowing you have no control, and the joy of sharing life with someone you love and who loves you. It doesn't mean you'll have no hardships, but it does mean you know you're never alone walking through those times of difficulty.

It manifests in the presence of his wisdom beyond knowledge, and the discernment to differentiate the wolves from the sheep and recognize their tactics. It evidences in the ability to look at old, painful memories without reexperiencing pain. Instead, you're able to see them through a new interpretation which sets you free from their power.

Surrendering into dependence also manifests as your spirit taking authority over your flesh, so the unhealthy urges of the flesh lose their powerful grip. We're better able to stand and fight, both against the flesh and against our wolves, because we know Jesus provides the power—if we take a stand.

I know my spiritual house is always in a state of needing cleaning. Our wolves are dogged in their relentless persistence. They have nothing to lose.

But Jesus' strength is made perfect in my weakness. He is "steadfastly resolved" (Isaiah 50:7b). His love "bears all things, believes all things, hopes all things, endures all things" and never fails (I Corinthians 13:7-8a). And when we pursue his Kingdom and his righteousness, he promises to give us everything else we need.

Questions

1. In what ways do you *follow* Jesus, and in what ways are you a *follower* of Jesus? How in your life do you evidence the characteristics of a follower as described by Paul?
2. How have you applied human wisdom (aka folly) to deal with struggles along your path? What were the consequences of your human wisdom? How have you utilized God's wisdom in your life? What were the results?
3. How is your spiritual "house cleaning" going? Where do you believe you are in the process?

4. In what ways have you tried to assimilate Jesus into your life? In what ways have you accommodated for Jesus in your life?
5. What manifestations of surrendering into dependence do you see in your life?

Prayer

Oh, my Jesus, how I love you! Thank you for helping me walk out what it means to be a follower, to clean my spiritual house, and to surrender into dependence. Jesus, the grip of dependence on my own knowledge is strong and shows up in so many ways—some more obvious than others. Please shine your light and reveal all the places where I still cling to my control and rely on my knowledge.

Jesus, I can't walk this path on my own. I need you. I'm tired of carrying the burden. I'm sick of believing the enemy's lies. I'm willing for you to step in and take over Lordship in my life. But I need your help to make it so. Help me see our relationship in a new light and create a new pattern of interaction and connection with you. I ask you to build that connection into oneness with you. Thank you, Lord, for accomplishing this. Amen.

Donna E. Lane, Ph.D.

THE WAY OF THE SHEPHERD

"The Lord is my shepherd. I lack nothing" (Psalm 23:1).

We close with a song.

One of the most familiar and oft memorized sections of Scripture is the 23rd psalm. The problem with familiarity is it breeds contempt, not in the sense of scorning the psalm—most people love this passage and find it beautiful—but contempt in the way of dismissal or disregard, as if we have nothing more to learn from these words. The words become rote, losing their meaning, like can happen with the Lord's Prayer and other, frequently repeated phrases or passages.

But I believe God's words are living, active, and penetrating, so I believe they always have something alive to say to us. So, let's look at the psalm with a fresh set of eyes and a heart open to listen to the Holy Spirit, applying everything we've discussed in the first seven chapters and bringing those ideas into practice as we seek revelation of God's words in this psalm.

"The Lord is my shepherd." (v. 1a).
Historians believe this psalm was written when David was king of all of Israel. In an interesting interplay of reality with

metaphor, the shepherd who became king called his King his shepherd.

David would've been familiar with the use of this metaphor in reference to the Lord, when Jacob called God his Shepherd from his deathbed and the Shepherd, the Rock of Israel as he spoke blessing and prophesy over his son, Joseph (Genesis 48:15, 49:24b). David also knew by the time of this writing that he had been called by God to be the shepherd of God's people, Israel (I Chronicles 11:2)—a shepherd called to shepherd people.

The imagery of a shepherd connotes care, provision, and protection. Unlike the image of a King, who lives separate from the people in his castle and sits above them on his throne, the imagery of a shepherd is intimate. The shepherd lives with the sheep. He guards them out on the fields, sleeping with them through the night. He brings them into his home when it is too cold or stormy to be outside. He walks among them and knows them, and they know him.

He tends them, which is not an easy task—sheep are high-maintenance. They are prone to infections, worms, parasites, and a myriad of other health problems. Their hooves must be trimmed, and their wool sheared. Sheep get very messy very quickly. Untangling their fleece can be nightmarish.

They graze seven hours a day, so providing adequately for their needs is a feat in itself. The shepherd also has to establish good boundaries, or sheep get themselves into trouble. Plus, predators can get to the sheep more readily without fencing to contain their wandering ways.

The shepherd has invested a lot of his resources to have his sheep, and they are of highest value to him. His sheep are the singular focus of his life. Also, the shepherd must pay close attention and care for each sheep individually, unlike a King who establishes laws and assumes his subjects will follow, never knowing any of them by name. Do you see why David chose the imagery of a shepherd?

Notice David uses, "my" shepherd, not "the" shepherd to describe the Lord. Their relationship is personal—one-on-one, as if David is the only sheep in the world.

"I lack nothing." (v. 1b).

"Enough" is the language of deprivation and lack. It's a hierarchical word, measuring against some standard. Think of how we use the word on a daily basis:

(Something) isn't good enough.
I don't have enough (of something).
That's good enough.
There's never enough (time, space, energy, money, etc.)
When will it be enough?

Do you see the unspoken standard and the lack reflected in these phrases?

We continuously measure ourselves and our circumstances, and find them coming up short of the mercurial, indeterminable standards we set. "I'm not good enough" is one of the most destructive lies to our relationship with God, telling us we must hold ourselves back from him until we get it together. It also assumes God is measuring us against some standard other than the presence of Jesus in our hearts.

God declared his creation is good, not good "enough" as if he looked around at his handiwork and found it didn't quite measure up to his expectations. He calls us "my delight" and beloved child, and says we are reverently and wonderfully made, holy and righteous in him. None of these words are hierarchical or measurement words. They speak to his and our identity.

What if, like control, "enough" is an illusion? David believed so. According to David, with our shepherd, there is no lack. He provides himself freely and fills us completely. Paul describes it this way: "If God is for us, who can be against us? Indeed, he who did not spare his own Son, but gave him up for us all—how will he not also, along with him, freely give us all things?" (Romans 8:31b-32). The fact that the Lord is our shepherd means by definition we lack nothing, because in him we already have all we need.

If we lack nothing, as David said, we have no reason to ever settle for less than God's best for us. So often, fear prompts us to settle, lest we be left with nothing. Afraid of regret later, we settle for the first thing we see. Fear of making the wrong decision also leads us to settle. "Good enough is better than nothing" is a common belief for those who live with a deprivation mindset.

Jesus had no place to lay his head, but he never held a deprivation mindset. He saw five loaves and a couple of fish and said, "You feed them." And the incredible abundance of God overflowed until 5000 were full—with leftovers.

If you find yourself using "not enough" language in reference to yourself or your circumstances, or you tend to settle for less than your true heart desires, deal with those beliefs as you would any lie. Take the belief to Jesus and seek his truth. You'll find Jesus speaking to your nature instead of your outcomes, and you'll realize two things: you are exactly who he made you to be, and he will give you the true desires of your heart.

"He takes me to lush pastures" (v. 2a).

Referring back to my description of tending the sheep, providing adequate grazing is part of the shepherd's provision. David says the shepherd doesn't leave the sheep to find pasture, he *takes* his sheep to the pasture—and not just any pasture, *lush* pastures, plural.

A sheep doesn't understand his needs. He is led by instinct and physical cravings. He wanders without any sense of direction or destination. He reacts more than responds. But when the shepherd takes him to what he really needs and provides in abundance, the sheep can live without worry or fear. He can enjoy the lush pastures without concern if there is "enough" because Jesus offers himself, and he is all.

The Hebrew words in this passage also have the connotation of rest. Many translations use the phrase "lie down in" to describe the sheep in the lush pastures. Because the worries of life are no longer burdens on us, and the fear of death no longer has power in us, we are able to "lie down" and find rest for our souls (Matthew 11:29b).

"He leads me to refreshing water" (v. 2b).
Shepherds watered their sheep beside wells, pulling up the water and filling their trough. Sheep need a lot of water, so the task of watering the sheep is a laborious, never-ending job. But Jesus describes a difference between his water and the water we pull up from a well:

> "If you had known the gift of God and who it is who said to you, 'Give me some water to drink,' you would have asked him, and he would have given you living water. Everyone who drinks some of this water will be thirsty again. But whoever drinks some of the water that I will give him will never be thirsty again, but the water that I will give him will become in him a fountain of water springing up to eternal life" (John 4:10, 13-14).

The woman to whom Jesus spoke had more than an empty water bucket. Her heart was hardened and hollow. She was scorned by her peers, treated as an outcast socially, and spurned by men. She had been ravaged by her circumstances. Her deep need for love was written all over her story.

Jesus saw beyond her sins and her hardness to the wounded heart of a little child. He offered her water that would heal her wounds and fill her heart with his love. Nothing is more refreshing and renewing than his living, eternal water.

Jesus offered her himself. Her response was to forget about her well water, shout for joy, and run to tell everyone about the man who truly knew her.

"He restores my strength" (v. 3a).
The imagery here is of a sheep who, through illness, predator attack, or mishap has become weakened, perhaps near the point of death. The good shepherd rescues the sheep from whatever pit he's fallen into, feeds the sheep in lush pastures, leads him to refreshing waters, and rebuilds his strength. The Hebrew word translated here as strength lends itself to a spiritual interpretation, meaning David wasn't referring to physical strength. He is pointing to how Jesus strengthens and restores our spirit from the harsh abuses of life in a fallen world.

Jesus also restores us to purity and righteousness by cleansing away the shame of our sins. His atoning death is the ransom payment freeing us from bondage, and "the blood of Jesus his Son cleanses us from all sin (I John 1:7b). So, in addition to food for our spirit and eternal living water, he restores us by his blood from our ill, weakened, and wounded state to holiness through his presence within us. As I Peter 5:10 states, "Christ will himself restore, confirm, strengthen, and establish you."

"He leads me down the right paths" (v. 3b).
What qualities does a good leader possess? Research has shown us that, first and foremost, good leaders lead by example. They know those they lead won't follow without trust, and if leaders haven't walked the path first, why would their followers trust them? In addition, if leaders expect us to do as they say, but they don't demonstrate what they say consistently in their behaviors, followers will bail because of their hypocrisy.

Good leaders offer encouragement, support, and guidance instead of criticism and control. Cooperative, collaborative work environments produce better than dictatorial or authoritarian styles of leadership.

Good leaders know the vision, mission, and goals and are committed and confident in them. They empower their followers and encourage them to use their strengths. The ability to reach into each follower and pull out the best from them so each member reaches their full potential is a valuable leadership skill. In order to do so, a leader must be able to see beyond the surface to the true nature of each person.

A good leader creates unity within the group, building strong bonds with and between members. Leaders who inspire, create energy in the group, and instill passion are the most effective. Excellent leaders focus on change and growth, wanting the best for their followers as well as for the group and the mission.

The best leaders serve those who follow them. They listen well and take care of their followers. In humility, they're able to share authority and tap into the expertise of those in their group while maintaining assurance in themselves and confidence in the vision and mission as a whole. They're able to hold out the vision in a way that their followers are all in and are willing to go all out.

Do these qualities remind you of someone?

Not only is Jesus the epitome of an excellent leader, he also knows the best direction to go. His way benefits his sheep and steers them away from harm. He will not lead his sheep into temptation.

He told us his path leads to life, but it's a narrow one. Without Jesus as our guide, none of us would find his path or be able to walk it. The broad road is an easier path to take, so many choose it, but Jesus warns the broad path leads to destruction.

What makes the broad path more attractive to us, even though it leads to our death? We're enticed by momentary pleasures and temporary gains and agree to exchange eternal joy for the tickle of fleshly gratification. It's as if we're taking a priceless pearl into a Dollar Store and buying useless plastic toys. Yes, we can play with the toys for a moment—until they fall apart—but like unknowing children, we don't recognize the value of the pearl.

Our sheep-ish flesh will insist on its desires unless our spirit takes authority over our flesh through the power of the Holy Spirit within us. When we surrender our human will and authority to God, his Spirit joins with ours to bring our flesh into submission. But if we hold onto some aspects of ourselves in an attempt to feel something is under our "control", our flesh will have its way. The more we try to "control" the more "out of control" we feel. Before we know it, we are well down the wide road and spiraling into our destruction.

Think of the narrow path as a trail across a ridgeline sided by two steep cliffs. If you've ever done any hiking, you know those sections of the trail are both difficult and beautiful. You get the best views from the top of the ridge, but you need to pay attention to your steps. One false step to the left or the right, and you're tumbling. How helpful it is to have a guide who knows the right path! He goes before us, takes us by the hand, and guards our steps so we can enjoy the view and not worry about falling.

"For the sake of his reputation" (v. 3b).
The literal translation of the Hebrew here is "for the sake of his name," but this translation better captures how the Jewish people of the time saw their name. Their name, or *shem,* spoke to their character. In this era, we might think of reputation as more of an issue of pride, which would change how we are reading this line, but we must understand the word choice in context. God isn't trying to protect his reputation for the sake of his pride. He is guarding our understanding of the quality of his character so we will know him in truth.

The Book of Job is, at its core, a challenge to God's character. Satan's question before God is essentially, "why does Job love you?" His first accusation of God is, "Job only loves you because of what he has. If I take away all he has, he'll curse your name." His second accusation is, "Job only loves you because he hasn't suffered. If I cause his body to suffer, he'll curse your name." Do you see here how "name" is synonymous with the character of God?

Satan's accusations are his judgments against God's character. He is suggesting God gives us things and protects us so we will love him. The truth is, God pours out his love on us *because* he loves us, not to get something back from us.

But how often is God presented in this light? We are easily tempted by the enemy to view God's character through a lens of pride, as if God is like us in needing affirmation of his being. We look at bad things happening to us as punishments from God, just like Job's friends when they were accusing Job of causing his own suffering through sin. We look at our suffering as failures by God, just like Job as he questioned why God had made him a target.

The ending of Job's story shows us why neither Satan nor Job's friends nor Job had any grounds to challenge God's character. God takes Job's why questions and Job's friends' human wisdom and Satan's accusations and turns them around by asking, "Do you know me? Do you know all I know? Do you see as I see? Do you know my character?"

God shows Job that why questions are not helpful questions. The correct question is, "*Who?*" Who created the beauty and splendor and majesty of this world? Who created the wild and wondrous creatures who live and die with no thought of *why?* Who is the source of all wisdom?

Even though why questions never bring peace, comfort, or healing, we still ask why bad things happen, don't we? We sometimes doubt God's love because of our circumstances. We question his faithfulness, his protection, and his care for us because we are looking at outcomes instead of looking to his character for understanding. We often fail to look for his redemption. We choose to pray for things to work out like we want them to instead of following Jesus' example in prayer and asking for God's will to be done.

When we lose sight of God's *character,* we lose sight of God. For our sakes, it is important for God to maintain his *shem* so we always know the quality of his character. Only then can we know how to interpret our life's circumstances in the light of truth.

"Even when I must walk through the darkest valley" (v. 4a)
David knows, both through his experience and wisdom from God, that we will all walk through dark valleys. We *must,* not necessarily because of our own choices but at the very least because of the fallen nature of this world.

We often understand suffering through a simplistic lens, where all suffering is in one big pot with one ingredient. In reality, suffering takes many forms and comes in different kinds with different labels. One kind of suffering comes from the consequences of our choices. Scripture refers to this type of suffering in this way: "A man reaps what he sows" (Galatians 6:7).

Another kind of suffering involves receiving consequences from the sins of others. Uriah is an example of this type of suffering as he died because of David's sinful desire for Bathsheba. A third kind of suffering comes through the fallen world. Paul explains it like this: "sin entered the world through one man, and death through sin, and in this way death came to all people" (Romans 5:12). We also experience suffering because of the writhing of the planet. The land itself is cursed by the fall and groans with disasters caused by the chaos of everything breaking down around us.

The type of suffering Jesus experienced, like the suffering of Job, is righteous suffering—suffering without apparent reason or cause, or unjust suffering. As I mentioned, we want a reason for our suffering. We want an answer to why. We want things to make sense. But righteous suffering has no explanation.

When we pile all suffering into one big pot, we're left in confusion, prompting those why questions that profit us nothing. But when we recognize the different types of suffering, we are better equipped to respond. Accepting suffering is inevitable shifts our focus from our circumstances to the presence of Jesus with us in the suffering. As he walks with us through the suffering, we find peace and comfort and healing in his arms.

David thought it important to write that we all *must* walk through the darkest valley. Perhaps he understood that facing the inevitability of suffering could motivate us to invest everything in our relationship with the shepherd. As Ecclesiastes 7:2b warns, "death is the destiny of every person, and the living should take this to heart."

For sheep, the darkest valley is the place of greatest threat. Wolves lurk and hunt in the darkness. Deep valleys afford many places for our wolves to hide in wait, and the sheep are easily surrounded and trapped. So, David is setting the stage with a worst-case scenario—the darkest valley where the sheep are most vulnerable and least able to protect themselves.

Yet, note the language David chose. He doesn't say trapped in the valley. He doesn't say he marches into the valley like a lamb to slaughter. He says he walks *through* the valley. Yes, the valleys are inevitable, but with Jesus going before us and living within us, we walk through even the darkest valleys and find redemption on the other side.

Prophesying about the coming Messiah, Isaiah wrote, "The people walking in darkness have seen a great light; on those living in the land of deep darkness a light has dawned" (Isaiah 9:2 NIV). After Jesus was tempted in the wilderness, he quoted these verses to initiate his ministry, and identified himself by these words. But we have no record indicating anyone heard and understood.

We have the benefit of being on the other side of history, where we know who Jesus is and why he came for us. Will we heed

David's words and walk with Jesus in the light, so when the darkest valley lies before us, we are ready for the journey through?

"I fear no danger" (v. 4b).

The presence of Christ's perfect love drives out fear. So, we don't run through the valley in panic. We don't flee through the valley in terror. We don't creep through the valley from rock to rock, looking over our shoulder, anxious and trembling. We *walk*, which connotes the calm, normal stride one would use in the broad daylight.

Jesus with us doesn't mean the wolves aren't in the valley. It doesn't mean the darkness of the valley doesn't impact us. But it does mean we have nothing to fear in the valley, no matter how dark it gets.

Evil is the greatest danger we face, but we have no reason to fear it. Evil's only threat is deception. As long as we live with Christ and believe his truth, we are not vulnerable to evil's tactics. However, we tend to focus on the threats to our physical bodies more than we concern ourselves with our spiritual wellbeing. If you compared the amount of time you spend on temporal concerns with the amount of time you spend on spiritual growth and maturity, which one wins out?

I don't say this to shame you. I believe we aren't aware of the discrepancy because we aren't paying attention—perhaps because evil distracts us or blinds us from what's happening. So, I want to bring it into the light and encourage you to invest your whole heart and mind and strength into your relationship with Christ. When the darkest valley comes upon you, you'll be glad you did.

"For you are with me" (v. 4c)

Once again, it is the presence of the shepherd in the darkest valley with us that makes a difference. He gets us through. He removes all reasons to fear. He redeems our journey. He goes before us and leads us on the right path. He gives us rest and provides for our needs. He is the one who makes a way for us.

David emphasizes the presence of the shepherd here by turning his psalm into a prayer. Now, he speaks to the shepherd directly, talking about what the shepherd does for him—perhaps by way of gratitude and praise.

David also emphasizes the personal nature of the shepherd's presence. He doesn't say, "God is with us." He says, "*You* are with *me*." As I said earlier, it's as if we are the only sheep in the world. He doesn't divide his time between his children. He doesn't have to. Because he is infinite, he can be fully present with me, and at the same time be fully present with you.

You've likely heard it said that if you were the only person in the world, Jesus would've still died for you. Usually, this statement is made in reference to the parable of the one lost sheep, where the shepherd leaves ninety-nine sheep in the pasture to go find the one sheep who is lost (Luke 15:4-7).

This parable isn't about Jesus leaving ninety-nine sheep behind. In the story, those sheep are safe in his pasture. The story was for the Pharisees, who were criticizing Jesus for eating with sinners. Jesus was speaking of pursuing the lost, and the joy in heaven when a sinner comes home. He wasn't saying he leaves the found, as if his sheep don't matter to him. Even when Jesus is pursuing the lost sheep, I know, as one of his found sheep, he is still right there with me. He never leaves me, just as he promised.

After all my years of intimate connection with Jesus, I'm still awestruck by the reality of his continuous, undivided attention. Because of this truth, I never have the feeling that I'm "bothering him" or "wasting his time"—something I've heard spoken by more Christians than I would hope—as if I have to prioritize which items I discuss with him based on their importance to him. But I've learned from him, if they're important to me, they *are* important to him.

Isn't that incredible?

As I sat by my son's bed, watching him take his final breaths, I felt him holding me. You're likely not surprised by that—such a significant event in my life, of course he'd be present, right? But I feel his presence the same when I'm in bed preparing myself to face a normal day, standing over the sink washing dishes, or sitting at my computer trying to decide the best word to convey something I'm trying to describe in one of my books.

It doesn't matter what I'm doing or if I'm doing nothing at all—he is with me.

"You rod and your staff reassure me" (v. 4d).

This verse has been twisted in so many ways, from suggesting the shepherd uses the rod to discipline his sheep since discipline produces a sense of security—so we should discipline our children in the same manner—to describing a shepherd using his staff to haul the sheep up from a ravine.

I believe, given the context of the shepherd's presence as the overarching message of this portion of the psalm, the message is simpler than that. David would've known the uses of a rod and a staff from his years tending sheep, but he didn't describe their purposes here. His focus was on the reassurance of the shepherd's presence.

The Hebrew word, *shaybet,* means a stick. A stick can be used in a variety of ways, but David didn't focus on how the stick was used. *Mishaynaw,* the word translated as staff, means a support. According to David, both tools are used to reassure the sheep. As they sense the touch of the shepherd, they are reminded their shepherd is with them, guarding them and guiding them.

In other words, he is saying, "I know my shepherd is always with me because I can feel the gentle touch of his staff. I'm reassured by my shepherd's presence because I know he has a rod to protect me from predators."

In the same way, because we hear the gentle voice of Jesus in our hearts or sense his gentle touch leading us or see the evidence of his handiwork in our lives, we are reassured of his continuous presence. We are never alone, left to the mercy of our wolves. Whether comforting us in the midst of grief and loss, guiding us through times of difficulty, or sharing with us during times of joy, we know Jesus, our shepherd, is always there.

"You prepare a feast before me" (v. 5a)

A feast is a time of celebration. I'm reminded of Jesus' parable of the compassionate father whose wayward son was lost to him. When the son came to his senses and returned, the father welcomed him home and prepared a feast to celebrate his return. And when the older brother complained about the celebration, the father replied, "'Son, you are always with me, and everything that belongs to me is yours. It was appropriate to celebrate and be glad, for your brother was dead, and is alive; he was lost and is found" (Luke 15:31-32).

This verse also brings to mind the feast at the wedding celebration of the Lamb, where the vast throng shouted, "Let us rejoice and exult and give him glory, because the wedding celebration of the Lamb has come, and his bride has made herself ready" (Revelation 19:7), and the angel exclaimed, "Blessed are those who are invited to the banquet at the wedding celebration of the Lamb!" (v. 9b).

As sheep of the shepherd, we are invited to the wedding celebration of the Lamb. We've been clothed in bright, clean, fine linen, made ready for the feast because of the sacrifice of Christ.

Notice that the shepherd is the one preparing the feast. He is the compassionate father celebrating the return of his wayward child. He is the bridegroom, preparing the feast to celebrate the coming of his bride.

Jesus told another parable about a wedding feast, one which a king prepared for his son. When everything was ready, the king sent his slaves to bring the invited guests, but they were indifferent and refused to come. Instead, they abused the king's slaves and killed them. In his anger, the king killed those men and burned their city.

Then, he sent the slaves out to invite everyone because the original invitees were unworthy. The wedding hall filled with guests. But the king saw someone who wasn't wearing wedding clothes and had him cast out into the darkness. The parable ends with the statement, "For many are called, but few are chosen" (Matthew 22:14).

The feast is prepared for the shepherd's sheep. All are invited to come to the feast, but those who have been clothed in clean linen because of the blood of the Lamb are the ones who will sit down at the table the shepherd has prepared. The feast celebrates his lost sheep who are found and made ready.

Once again, the feast is a personal experience, as David says it is prepared "before me." In other words, the celebration is prepared for each individual sheep. Imagine Jesus and you, sitting together at a table with a feast spread before you, all to celebrate *you*. Do you know you are that important to him?

You are.

"In plain sight of my enemies" (v. 5b).

Now, here is a strange twist. You might imagine the feast would be prepared in a banquet hall, where the doors are shut and only those invited could enter—where it's obvious the sheep are safe. But as in the parable of the king's wedding feast, both good and bad are invited to come in. The table is laid out in the valley surrounded by wolves.

Do you sense the indifference of the shepherd toward the wolves? He isn't trying to hide you or secret away the food of the feast. He's not telling you to hurry up and eat so he can get you out of there. He simply doesn't care if they watch the feast. "In plain sight" indicates a brazen, bold statement to the wolves—"this is my sheep, and you can't have them!" He's not worried in the least. Why should we be?

But this statement is also a picture of how we live our lives. We are always in the presence of our enemies. But the constant presence of our shepherd renders that fact irrelevant. Their threat is neutralized when we are one with the shepherd. We can enjoy the celebration feast without fear, knowing our wolves are lurking in the trees—yet, reassured we are safe in the hands of the shepherd.

"You refresh my head with oil" (v. 5c)
Anointing with oil symbolized sanctification (Exodus 30:22-31). Whatever or whoever was anointed with the oil was set apart as holy. The oil was originally meant for the priests and the tabernacle but was later used to anoint kings as well.

Now, we are set apart and made holy by the Holy Spirit. Do you recall the parable of the ten virgins? The oil for their lamps represents the Holy Spirit within us, who prepares us for the coming of the bridegroom. So, in our case, our anointing is not just at the feast. It is a continuous anointing, a constant presence within us, cleansing us, refreshing us, and renewing us.

By the anointing oil of the Holy Spirit, we are continuously transformed until we reflect the likeness of Christ. We are made holy, not by our efforts to achieve holiness or righteousness, but by *his* holiness and righteousness. His truth moves our hearts closer to his and makes us whole.

As I John 2:27 explains, "Now as for you, the anointing that you received from him resides in you, and you have no need for anyone to teach you. But as his anointing teaches you about all things, it is true and is not a lie. Just as it has taught you, you reside in him." We have one teacher, who is Christ. His Spirit teaches us and leads us into all truth. And as he lives in us, we also live in him. We are made one.

"My cup is completely full" (v. 5d).

Two kinds of cups are presented in Scripture. The first is the cup of God's wrath and judgment. Throughout the Old Testament prophets and in Revelation, this cup is described as filled with wine the people are forced to drink until they are drunk and vomit. Jesus mentions "the cup that the Father has given" (John 18:11b), meaning the pouring out of God's judgment on Jesus for the sins of the world.

The other cup is the cup of Christ, filled with the blood of Jesus, poured out for many for the forgiveness of sin. This cup represents the new covenant, God's promise to redeem us from bondage to sin. When we take this cup during Communion, we are told to remember what Christ has done for us. Instead of God's wrath, this cup is the symbol of God's love for his children.

I find it very interesting that the cup of God's forgiveness and love was made known to David well before Jesus came. Similarly, if you read Psalm 22, you'll see David was shown Christ's crucifixion before it occurred. The accuracy of the detail he shares is stunning.

David is describing being filled with the shepherd's presence and love to the point where nothing is lacking, pointing the reader back to his opening lines. Not one drop is missing. David has everything he needs. God's provision is complete.

The same is true for us. In our oneness with Christ, us in him and him in us, we have everything we need. The shepherd fills us to the brim with his forgiveness, his love, and his truth. We may stand in the darkest valley, encircled by wolves, but we are surrounded by his light, fed at his table, and filled with his presence. As David proclaims in Psalm 16:11, "You lead me in the path of life. I experience absolute joy in your presence; you always give me sheer delight."

"Surely your goodness and faithfulness will pursue me all my days" (v. 6a).

This verse centers on God's *khesed*. Alternately translated as mercy, compassion, love, grace, devotion, loyalty, favor, and faithfulness, this word encompasses so much more than any of these words can convey. Our language has no equivalent.

Khesed means a steadfastness of love beyond love. It is persistent, unwavering, and unconditional. This love includes action on behalf of the loved one for their benefit, even though the love is undeserved. *Khesed* intervenes on the loved one's behalf, pursues them through the darkness, and rescues them from harm. All of the attributes of God are summarized in this one word. It is God-love unlike any other.

Khesed sent Jesus willingly to the cross to die in our place. God pursued Israel across the centuries and never gave up on them, despite their many betrayals, because of *khesed*. The depth and richness of this kind of love can't be described—it can only be understood through the experience of it.

When I shook my fist at God in anger until my despair collapsed me face down on the floor, I experienced *khesed* for the first time. He reached out his hand to me, and his indescribable love flowed over me like an ocean wave. I was immersed in him completely. I deserved rejection, or at least chastisement for my insolence. Yet, he continued to pursue me, just as David described in this verse. And he embraced me without hesitation or limit, despite my behavior toward him.

David is certain of God's *khesed* and expresses this assurance in the first word of the verse. The verb, *radaf,* translated pursue, creates an interesting word picture. The word is most often used to describe an enemy chasing down a retreating army, or wolves running down prey. In fact, this is the only place in Scripture where this word is used in reference to God's love. To choose this verb focuses on the relentless nature of God's pursuit of his children. He chases us down to the ends of the earth and the end of our lives, and he will *never stop.*

Khesed is the kind of love that fills you beyond your ability to contain it. His *khesed* is what awakens our hearts and enlivens our spirits. It enables us to love him. It empowers us to love others as he loves us. It heals our brokenness from living in a fallen world. It makes us whole and complete.

I picture Moses, his face radiant after being in God's presence—so much so, he had to cover himself with a veil because of the fear the Israelites felt seeing God's glory on his face. I think about Jesus, radiant in his true being while Peter, James, and John trembled in fear at the base the mountain. I read Paul talking about how we, now with unveiled faces, also reflect the glory of the Lord as we are transformed into his image. And I realize the light of God's glory is his *khesed,* now reflected in us as his Spirit lives in us and flows through us into the world.

"And I will live in the LORD's house for the rest of my life." (v. 6b).

We are invited to the shepherd's banquet as guests, but we are embraced as children. Like the shepherd brings his sheep into his home to sleep when the weather grows harsh, we are brought into our shepherd's dwelling as part of his family.

Many read this verse and interpret it as referring to our eternal heavenly home, which it does. But notice David's language. His dwelling with the Lord begins in the present and continues from this point forward. He doesn't say, "I will dwell in the house of the Lord someday." He is saying I will dwell in the Lord's house from now on.

Jesus told his disciples, "There are many dwelling places in my Father's house. Otherwise, I would have told you, because I am going away to make ready a place for you. And if I go and make ready a place for you, I will come again and take you to be with me, so that where I am you may be too" (John 14:2-3). Jesus was going away to prepare our dwelling, but if David's dwelling was present during his life, where did Jesus go to prepare this dwelling?

I believe Jesus is referring to his dwelling place in our hearts. Like the revelation given to David about Christ's crucifixion and the cup of his love and forgiveness, David appears to have received special insight into the coming of the Holy Spirit to live in our hearts.

Jesus prepares our hearts as his dwelling by going before us to cleanse us of the shroud of our lies and the shame of our sin. His *khesed* flows through us like a purifying flood of holy water and anointing oil. Our heavenly residence doesn't begin when we die. It begins the day Jesus moves in. Once he makes the dwelling place ready—meaning he returns us to our true, created nature and connects us back to ourselves—then he takes us with him to that dwelling. We live in his Kingdom from that day forward.

So, God's Kingdom is within us, where the shepherd lives. It is a here-and-now reality and an eternal reality. The only way to his dwelling is by his Spirit. He *is* the way.

Throughout this book, we've looked at Christ's nature as our shepherd and our nature as his sheep. Psalm 23 encapsulates everything we've discussed:
    his provision, covering all of our needs;
    rest for our souls;
    living water, springing up to eternal life;
    his strength in our weakness;
    his guidance and leadership on the right paths;
    his concern for our best interests in all things;
    his continuous presence;
    how he walks with us through times of darkness;
    his love which casts out our fear;
    his gentle care;
    the ways he provides reassurance of his presence;
    the invitation to be his bride;

the celebration of our coming home to him;
his response to our enemies;
the anointing oil of his Spirit to sanctify us and make us holy;
the filled cup of forgiveness for our sins;
his unsurpassed, never-failing *khesed* love;
his dwelling place with us;
our oneness with Christ.

As you read Psalm 23 and consider its deeper meanings, I pray you find yourself better equipped to walk in the way of the shepherd. I pray your spirit is filled to the brim with the shepherd's *khesed* and you shine with his radiant glory. I pray your Kingdom dwelling begins now. And I pray you experience oneness with Christ in such a way that your every thought, your every step, your every breath, your every heartbeat matches his.

Questions

1. What does the phrase, "The Lord is my shepherd" mean to you now?
2. In what ways do you see the Lord's guidance leading you? How has he shown you his presence in your darkest valleys?
3. Which son of the compassionate father are you most like? How do you feel about God's celebration feast being held in the presence of your wolves?
4. When and how have you experienced God's *khesed*?
5. How do you experience oneness with Christ?

Prayer

My Jesus, I have no words to describe how much your love means to me. You know my heart. You hear the songs of my spirit and the cries of my soul. Fill me with your love until my cup overflows. Let your glory shine on my face. Keep my feet on your paths. Surround me with your light to push back the darkness in the valley and hold off my wolves. Prepare me with clothes of white linen to sit at the wedding feast with the bridegroom. Purify me with your anointing oil. Lead me to places of rest and cleanse me with springs of living water.

You are my shepherd, and I am your sheep. You are my all. Please, my dear Jesus, make us one. In your holy name I pray, Amen.

OTHER TITLE BY THIS AUTHOR

Fiction

The Interview
Sky Light Falls: Whisperers Book One
Sky Light Rises: Whisperers Book Two
Sky Light Ends: Whisperers Book Three
This Hallowed Ground
Time Forgotten: Cleansed Prequel
Coming soon: Infidel Wars: Cleansed Book One

Nonfiction

Restored Christianity
Wilderness Meditations
Strength in Adversity
Strength in Our Story
Seeking Treasures
Dwelling
Recognizing Jesus: A Study of the Gospel of Mark

Professional

Please Share the Door: I'm Freezing—Creating Oneness in Marriage
Trauma Narrative Treatment
Gold Stone

Children's

God Knows All About You
Where is God
In Search of Sparkle: A Faerie Fairy Tale

How to Connect

Websites— https://thedoctorslane.com
https://restoredchristianity.com
https://codylanefoundation.com
Facebook: https://facebook.com/Dr.Donna.E.Lane
https://facebook.com/groups/madeforanotherworld
Twitter—@Doctordelane
Instagram—@doctordelane
LinkedIn— https://www.linkedin.com/in/doctordelane/
YouTube Channel:
https://www.youtube.com/channel/UC4HPDj1urH5FvSmXucqdTXQ

Sign up for my newsletter for TWO FREE BOOKS!
https://thedoctorslane.com/sign-up

Donna E. Lane, Ph.D.

ABOUT THE AUTHOR

As an award-winning author, Christian counselor, spiritual director, and professor of counseling, I use my experience and professional insight into human motivations and personalities to develop complex characters and explore difficult psychological topics in-depth.

My books range from imaginings of other worlds and futuristic societies to profound explorations of deep theological concepts. They offer new perspectives, challenge in-depth self-examination, and encourage a fearless embrace of life's joys and sorrows. I take you to other worlds and other times. I tackle difficult questions. I face genuine suffering and rejoice in God's redemption. After you finish my books, I hope you find yourself enlivened and enriched, with a newfound desire to experience God to the fullest.

My husband, David, and I enjoy working and writing together. Our passion is to help others explore and deepen their relationship with Jesus Christ, and our work and our writings are geared toward that goal.

Our children are grown with families of their own. Our son, Hayden, is a teacher, married to Natalie, a nurse. They have two children, Coen and Petra, our precious grandchildren. Our daughter, Lindsey, is a veterinarian, married to Kyle, an electrical engineer.

Our youngest son, Cody, passed away at the age of seventeen from a degenerative neurological disorder. His life stands as a beautiful reflection of what it means to live in the Kingdom of God in the here-and-now. His life story informs much of my writing.

www.ingramcontent.com/pod-product-compliance
Lightning Source LLC
Chambersburg PA
CBHW051343040426
42453CB00007B/380